THE JOHN HARVARD LIBRARY

Bernard Bailyn
Editor-in-Chief

COIN'S FINANCIAL SCHOOL

By

WILLIAM H. HARVEY

Edited by Richard Hofstadter

THE BELKNAP PRESS OF
HARVARD UNIVERSITY PRESS
Cambridge, Massachusetts
1963

Distributed in Great Britain by Oxford University Press, London

Library of Congress Catalog Card Number 63–20768

Printed in the United States of America

CONTENTS

Coin's Financial School and the Mind of "Coin" Harvey, by Richard Hofstadter 1

A Note on the Text 81

COIN'S FINANCIAL SCHOOL

Preface 89

Chapter I. 93

The first day. The money unit. The first interruption. Young Scott returns. The crime of 1873.

Chapter II. THE SECOND DAY 113

The ratio. Their commercial values compared. A comparison for 200 years. Mr. Gage makes an admission. Quantity of gold and silver. A real estate man asks a question. Changing ratio.

Chapter III. THE THIRD DAY 135

Silver and gold adopted. An interruption. Money as a science. General Principles. Our financial and credit system.

Chapter IV. THE FOURTH DAY 159

A day of questions. The Latin Union. Supt. of Mails asks a question. Cost of producing silver. A greenbacker. Money based on labor. No special advantage to silver states. Professors of political economy. Improved facilities. The tariff proposition. Mayor Hopkins asks a question.

CONTENTS

Chapter V. THE FIFTH DAY 185

Quantitative theory of money. Quantity of gold in the world. Measuring the gold. Quantity of silver in the world. Changing the measure. An illustration. Another illustration. The debts of the world.

Chapter VI. THE SIXTH DAY 217

Independent free coinage.

Coin Receives 240

Appendix 247

Index 251

INTRODUCTION

Coin's Financial School and the Mind of "Coin" Harvey

COIN'S FINANCIAL SCHOOL

AND THE MIND OF "COIN" HARVEY

Who today can understand without a strenuous effort of imagination the passions once aroused by the cry for free silver? Despite the pointless and long sustained policy of silver purchases into which the federal government was forced by silver interests in 1934, the once heated issue of the bimetallic standard has been rendered obsolete by modern devices of monetary management. Yet a whole generation of Americans was embroiled from the 1870's to the 1890's in the argument over silver. To the combatants of that era, silver and gold were not merely precious metals but precious symbols, the very substance of creeds and faiths which continued long afterward to have meaning for men living on the echoes of nineteenth-century orthodoxies. In 1933, when Franklin D. Roosevelt took the United States "off gold," Lewis W. Douglas said, at the end of a long and anxious night, "This is the end of Western civilization." From another point of view, Senator Ashurst of Arizona, pressed by Secretary Morgenthau about his persistence on silver, replied: "My boy, I was brought up from my mother's knee on silver and I can't discuss that with you any more than you can discuss your religion with me."[1]

[1] Raymond Moley, *After Seven Years* (New York, 1939), pp. 159–160; John M. Blum, *From the Morgenthau Diaries* (Boston, 1959), p. 186.

The free silver campaign of 1896 was one of the stormy, disruptive campaigns of our history, the first since Jackson's day when a presidential election hung on a financial issue. Sentiment for free coinage of silver was not strong enough to elect Bryan, but it was strong enough to wrest control of the Democratic party away from President Cleveland, to split the Republicans into two irreconcilable factions, and to transform the new Populist party into a single-issue satellite of Bryan and the Democrats. It was menacing enough to unite all the forces of goldbug respectability behind McKinley, and to spur an election effort without precedent in our history. In defeating silver the goldbugs were not merely defeating a reform, they were stemming a crusade.

The student who tries to recapture the emotions of this crusade reads Bryan's "Cross of Gold" speech as the great document of the silver cause. Yet this speech sums up a case already made; it assumes much and explains little to a reader ignorant of the preceding years of monetary argument. One cannot tell from it how the silver men arrived at their sense of conviction. If Bryan was immediately understood by his audience, it was because he played upon a set of feelings already formed and inflamed by a vast literature of analysis and agitation; and of all this literature, by far the most effective and memorable work was William Hope Harvey's little book of 155 pages, first printed two years before, in June 1894.

Eighteen ninety-four was a grim year. A depression had begun sharply early in 1893. Its effects were heightened by a stock market panic in May and by the threatened exhaustion of federal gold reserves. By mid-1894 the economy was in its full grip. Farmers were frantic over the collapse of wheat and cotton prices.

Bank failures and business bankruptcies mounted to unimagined heights. Thousands of men of substance found themselves ruined, as Henry Adams knew when he lamented that his entire generation had had notice to quit. Mills and factories were closing daily, and soon one man of every five in the labor force was unemployed. Long lines of hungry and desperate men tramped the streets and highways. While Harvey was getting *Coin's Financial School* ready for publication, Coxey's "army" of unemployed was marching in protest on Washington, and in the month the book appeared the violent Pullman strike began, which was soon to be smashed by Federal troops sent to Illinois by President Cleveland. By the end of 1894 Cleveland's party was quarreling irreconcilably about his fiscal policies, and the Populist party, which some conservatives looked upon as the vanguard of an anarchistic apocalypse, had made serious inroads on the strength of both major parties in the West and South. No one knew how far the crisis would carry the country from its old ways, or how many institutions were still fated to crumble.

Sufferers from the crisis were crying for a simple solution, and their confusion over its causes only heightened their dogmatism about its cure. The dispute over the government's silver purchases, a central issue since 1890, had fixed everyone's mind on the money question, and the near exhaustion of the Treasury's gold reserves commanded nervous day-by-day attention. Almost everyone was either denouncing the free silver maniacs of the West and South or scourging the bankers and Shylocks of New York and London. *Coin's Financial School* rode on the wave of an almost unbelievable money mania. A correspondent wrote to Cleveland's secretary in May 1895: "Have been pretty well over the country since we last met, traveling through twenty-four States, more than ten thousand miles, South and West. The people in that section are simply crazy on the money question; they cannot discuss it rationally." A rural editor in Kentucky wrote: "Politics down here has gone mad. Every crank in the country is loose and nothing less than a stone wall will stop them." Kenesaw M. Landis reported from Illinois:

> The God's truth is the Democratic party in Indiana and Illinois is wildly insane on this subject . . . The farmers are especially unruly . . . I've got a lot of farmer uncles down in Indiana—good honest and intelligent men as honesty and intelligence go at this day—but utterly wild on the money question. You can't do anything with them — just got to let them go.

A Mississippi Congressman wrote to Cleveland's Secretary of War in April 1895: "A little free silver book called 'Coin's Financial School' is being sold on every railroad train by the newsboys and at every cigar store . . . It is being read by almost everybody."[2]

ii

For a long time now only a few specialists have read this little tract that was once read by "almost everybody." Although printed in the hundreds of thousands, it is hard to come by, and its yellowing pages crack and crumble as they are turned. No doubt thousands of frail copies were simply read and thumbed to death. But neither Harvey nor his pamphlet can be forgotten. He was the Tom Paine of the free silver movement, and *Coin's Financial School* was to the silver men of 1896 what *Common Sense* had been to the revolutionaries of

[2] James A. Barnes, *John G. Carlisle, Financial Statesman* (New York, 1931), pp. 449, 452, 438.

1776. That free silver was a losing cause should not blind us to the importance of *Coin's Financial School* as a basic expression of the American popular imagination.

Bryan remarked of *Coin's Financial School* that it was "the most potent of educational forces at work in behalf of bimetallism. It is safe to say that no book in recent times has produced so great an effect in the treatment of an economic question." No one will ever know how many copies were distributed. Harvey wrote to *The Forum* in 1895 that sales during its first eleven months exceeded 400,000 copies. During the campaign of 1896, the National Silver Party bought and distributed 125,000 copies. The most conservative estimate of its sales is 650,000, the most generous is Harvey's of 1,500,000. His widow's more sober guess of 1,000,000 seems closer to the mark, and is by no means implausible.[3] Priced variously at 25 cents, 50 cents, and a dollar, published in varying grades of paper and binding, bought in quantities by interested organizations, and widely hawked about by vendors, *Coin's Financial School* was susceptible to a mass circulation reached often in its day by popular magazines but seldom by books.

The literary form chosen for Harvey's presentation of his ideas was simple but effective. "Coin," a young but preternaturally wise little financier, tries to remedy the sufferings of the depression by attacking the intellectual illusions which have brought it about. He establishes a school in Chicago at the Art Institute, to which he invites the young men of the city for a series of six lectures on the money question. The book reports

[3] Bryan, *The First Battle* (Chicago, 1896), pp. 153–154, 292; *The Forum*, 19 (July, 1895), 573n; Frank L. Mott, *Golden Multitudes: The Story of Best Sellers in the United States* (New York, 1947), pp. 170–171. In *Coin's Financial School Up to Date* (Chicago, 1895), p. i, Harvey mentioned sales of 5,000 a day.

his lectures, but since he is occasionally interrupted by friendly or argumentative questions, it takes the form of a monologue broken by occasional dialogues. (Harvey may have been led to this dramatic device by the example of his first publication, Archbishop Walsh's tract on bimetallism, which was presented as an interview with a reporter.) As the lectures go on, the audience supposedly fills with actual persons whom Harvey did not scruple to name; a few are obscure friends of the silver cause, but they are mainly well-known editors, politicians, businessmen, lawyers, and economists. The fictitious Coin thus appears to engage in real encounters, heard attentively by men like Philip D. Armour, Marshall Field, H. H. Kohlsaat, and Senator Shelby Cullom.[4] Gold advocates pose questions which they are confident will trip Coin, but he answers with such a majestic command of fact and theory that they are thrown into confusion. Among those most decisively worsted are the leading Chicago banker, Lyman J. Gage, later to be McKinley's Secretary of the Treasury, and the monetary authority, J. Laurence Laughlin, Professor of Economics at the University of Chicago. The introduction of these actual contemporaries gave the "school" such an air of reality, despite the patently fictional character of its central figure, that many readers believed that the lectures had actually been given. Laughlin, who was particularly outraged at having been portrayed as worsted by a tyro in economics, found it desirable, along with Gage, Kohlsaat, and some of the others allegedly in attendance at the "school," who had grown tired of answering letters from

[4] In an hour spent with contemporary directories one can identify most of the persons named in *Coin's Financial School.* However, there was no such person as "young Medill" (p. 99), and it is possible that a few other names were also erroneous.

readers querying them about what they were supposed to have said, to join in a statement that the whole thing was a fiction.

Though Laughlin believed that an amateur work like Harvey's was "not worthy of serious discussion," he found it necessary to answer Harvey in a pamphlet, *Facts about Money*, and even to debate with him on a public platform. Another of the well-known authors who refuted Harvey was Horace White, the economic journalist of the New York *Evening Post*, and the author of a standard work on money and banking, who called his onslaught *Coin's Financial Fool: or The Artful Dodger Exposed. A Complete Reply to Coin's Financial School.* The rage for monetary argument and the extraordinary success of Harvey's little book provoked a host of answers by goldbug opponents — and the literature mounted to a point which would make a major project for a bibliographer.[5] The answers were written with varying degrees of economic sophistication and provided with titles of varying flippancy or solemnity: for example, George E. Roberts's *Coin at School in Finance*, Edward Wisner's *Cash vs. Coin*, Jay Loring's *Coin's Financial School Exposed and Closed*, Robert F. Rowell's *The Mistakes of Coin*, John A. Frazer's and Charles H. Serghel's *Sound Money*, Melville D. Landon's *Money, Gold, Silver, or Bimetallism*, John F. Cargill's *A Freak in Finance*, Stanley Wood's *An-*

[5] Some of the leading items in this literature were reviewed in Willard Fisher's judicious and valuable essay, "'Coin' and His Critics," *Quarterly Journal of Economics*, 10 (January 1896), 187–208. Harvey expressed his view of the critics of his book when he said that they were "slaves set to lash the author of that book and their master is—money." Christ, he said, had been killed at the behest of the money-changers of Judea, and now he, Harvey, was being persecuted by the same "unconquered and relentless" money power. "'Coin's Financial School' and its Censors," *North American Review*, 161 (July 1895), 72, 74–75.

swer to "Coin's Financial School," W. B. Mitchell's *Dollars or What?*, L. G. Power's *Farmer Hayseed in Town: or, The Closing Days of Coin's Financial School,* Charles Elton Blanchard's *Report of Uncle Sam's Homilies in Finance,* Everett P. Wheeler's *Real Bi-Metallism or True Coin versus False Coin.* Yet not one of these appears to have had even a small portion of the impact of the book it was meant to refute.

These titles evoke the atmosphere of an age of polemics; yet perhaps the most remarkable thing about *Coin's Financial School* is the comparative austerity of its tone. To be sure, it has its flashes of sardonic humor, its strokes of dazzling irrelevancy, and its moments of headlong rhetoric. But on the whole, when one considers Harvey's own mettlesome temperament and remembers the intemperance of a time when the gold-bug press frequently described silver Senators as "fanatics," "cossacks," "border ruffians," "bandits," "disloyalists," "traitors," and "lunatics," *Coin's Financial School* seems the more remarkable for an air, however delusive, of sticking to the task of rational analysis. It has behind it the fierce logic of the one-idea mind, the firm conviction that complex social issues can be unravelled to the last point and pinned down for good, that social problems can really be solved, and solved by simple means. However amateur and unsure, it is a rather technical discussion of one of the most intricate of subjects, the monetary standard; and one can only be touched at the thought of the effort of mind that it must have called forth in many of its readers, who hoped that by reading it carefully they might *understand* what had happened. Probably more than any other of our politico-social best sellers, it makes a primarily ratiocinative demand on its readers. Compared with our other popular tracts on social issues, its appeal is hard to comprehend — it lacks the great revolutionary rhetoric of Paine's *Common Sense,* the alluring pornographic overtones of the widely read anti-Catholic pamphlet, *The Awful Disclosures of Maria Monk*, the human appeal of *Uncle Tom's Cabin*, the major prophetic gifts and sustained analysis of *Progress and Poverty*, the novelistic form and universal significance of *Looking Backward*. It stays close to details of the money problem, relying mainly upon effective cartoons for its emotional impact. For Harvey himself it was the product of a rare moment. Nothing that he wrote afterward was to have anything like its argumentative surge or its show of coherence. Nothing that he had done before gave any hint that he would be known to the world as the author of a book.

iii

William Hope ("Coin") Harvey was born in 1851 in the little village of Buffalo, in the western part of Virginia, the fifth child of six born to Robert and Anna Harvey.[6] Robert Trigg Harvey was a Virginian of Scottish and English ancestry, and his wife, who had Virginian ancestors traceable to colonial times, was descended also from French stock that had long since peopled the territory around nearby Gallipolis. Almost nothing is known of William Harvey's childhood except that it was disturbed by conflict between the Unionist majority in his region and secessionist sympathizers, among whom were some members of his father's family. One of young Harvey's sisters was sent to a convent for safety's sake

[6] Biographical information, except where otherwise indicated, is taken from Jeannette P. Nichols' excellent sketch, "Bryan's Benefactor: Coin Harvey and his World," *Ohio Historical Quarterly*, 67 (October 1958), 299–325.

during the war, and, to the family's distress, became a nun. An older brother was wounded fighting under Lee.

At the war's end, young Harvey began study at the little academy in Buffalo, taught school for a few months at the age of sixteen, and afterward briefly attended Marshall College, then a state normal school offering instruction at the secondary school level. His three months there marked the end of his formal eduction. He spent a short time reading law, in those days the customary way of preparing for the profession, was admitted to the bar at the age of nineteen, and opened practice in the village of Barboursville, West Virginia, the seat of Cabell County. When the railroad tycoon, Collis P. Huntington, established a depot for the Chesapeake and Ohio railroad at the Ohio River town which was named for him, William Hope Harvey made the first of his many adult changes of residence and entered practice in partnership with an older brother in Huntington, West Virginia. The town, which was growing rapidly, was the largest place in which Harvey had lived.

Before long, Harvey's restlessness had him on the move. In 1875, at the age of twenty-four, he moved to Gallipolis, Ohio, a busy spot in the Ohio River Valley about forty miles above Huntington, and there met Anna Halliday whom he married in 1876. The couple soon went to Cleveland, where Harvey tried his hand at law in a major center of commerce and industry and where the first two of their four children were born.[7] After three years in Cleveland, Harvey took his growing family to Chicago, but a little more than a year of Chicago was enough for him, and in 1881 the Harveys, now numbering

[7] Since Ohio was a center of Greenback agitation during the 1870's, it is quite possible that Harvey first became interested in the money question during these years.

five, returned to Gallipolis, where Harvey became attorney for several wholesale houses in Ohio. In 1883 a client's affairs took him to the southwest corner of Colorado, where prospectors had not long before made rich silver discoveries, and there, at the age of thirty-two, Harvey had his first experience with the white metal that was to give him his place in history. The following year he took his family, along with a force of ten young workers, to Colorado, where he started working claims near Ouray, and where the young entrepreneur's still growing family was housed in a large mountainside cabin. In the cold of winter, his wife and children moved to California, while the young father stayed at the mines, except for Christmas time, living near his work in a room fashioned out of one corner of an engine house. For three years Harvey worked arduously, and at some cost to his health, superintending the production of "The Silver Bell," a mine of considerable yield. But he had entered silver mining at one of its worst moments. High costs of operation were driving out small enterprisers and favoring large producers. The mine fields swarmed with displaced workers, wages fell, and the industry was riven with strikes. Worst of all, silver prices, which had gone down disastrously in the 1870's, were still falling sharply as production rose.

Harvey soon abandoned the mines for the real estate business, which he combined with his law practice. This occupied him for six years successively in Pueblo, Denver, and Ogden, Utah. He was remembered in Colorado for having sold an "Elixir of Life," which was curative of a variety of human ills, and as one of the promotors of an exposition hall in Pueblo, the "Mineral Palace," which housed a collection of Rocky Mountain minerals. Opened with a grand fete in the summer of 1890, the palace was the most gaudy and the most successful of the various enterprises with which Harvey had been associated. The taste of success did not overcome Harvey's wanderlust, for his moves to Denver and Ogden followed his ventures in Pueblo. In Ogden he bought and improved a house, perhaps with permanent settlement in mind. He also bought for development a one-mile frontage along Great Salt Lake, and appears to have tried to promote a festival patterned after the New Orleans Mardi Gras, in which local tradition reports that he lost a substantial sum.

In any case Harvey had enough capital left to move his brood back to Chicago again in May 1893 and to set up a specialized publishing business dedicated to free silver. At forty-two he was neither a complete failure nor, in his ambitious terms, a success. His restless search for wealth had led him to take up nine residences in the thirteen years since he had begun the practice of law. He had been in Colorado long enough to feel the anguish and disappointment of the silver miners and to absorb the historical and monetary lore of the free silver advocates, which was as much an orthodoxy in Colorado as the gold standard was in New York. Untutored in the intricacies of academic economics, he had absorbed in a bitter school of experience the convictions that were to bring into focus the major discontents of his time. "Coin" Harvey was prepared for his sudden leap onto the stage of history.

iv

"Coin" Harvey was a money crank, one of a type the United States has produced in considerable numbers. The early demand for an adequate money supply, the perennial want of an adequate central banking system, the open character of our entrepreneurial system, the violent upheavals and reversals of individual fortunes — all these things have produced a great many economic dissenters and have given their homemade systems of ideas a wide reception. Each depression has been a prolific breeder of panaceas, panacea mongers, and monetary pamphleteers. The striking thing about the depression of the nineties was how rapidly the cry for free coinage of silver shoved other reform proposals from the center of the stage.

To understand this, one must recall briefly the history of monetary issues since the Civil War. Before the war, the United States had been in law (though not, as we shall see, in fact) on a bimetallic standard. In 1861, wartime demands forced the country to suspend specie redemption of its currency and to issue United States notes, the "greenbacks," which were full legal tender, except for the payment of customs duties and interest on the public debt. The nation was now on an inconvertible paper standard. Its greenbacks circulated at a substantial and growing discount in terms of gold. A period of hectic inflation ensued, and when the war was over, many economic and political leaders urged that the greenbacks be retired and that specie payments be promptly resumed. They met with a good deal of resistance from farmers and many businessmen, particularly in the West, who remembered wartime inflation for the prosperity that accompanied it, who had already suffered from the postwar economic relapse, and who dreaded any further currency contraction. (There were also some high-tariff businessmen, East and West, who favored inflation because it would have a protectionist effect.)

Postwar inflationism, then, first took the form of resistance to the retirement of the greenbacks. Superficially, this movement had a moment of success in 1868, when Congress prohibited the further retirement and cancellation of greenbacks, and another such moment in 1874, when under the stress of depression, Congress somewhat increased the number of these bills. Indeed, during the depression that began in 1873, greenback inflationism waxed strong. A new Greenback party arose, whose candidates amassed a million votes in the Congressional elections of 1878.

But, so far as the price level itself was concerned, the inflationists had been fighting a losing battle since 1865. The men who directed American policy during these years were following a spartan policy. They believed that the currency would not be sound or stable until the government returned to specie payments — more specifically, until it restored, at full value, the gold dollar that had prevailed before the war. In order that this be accomplished, it was necessary that the American price level fall in relation to European price levels — which were themselves falling. Otherwise, high American prices would have lowered exports, increased imports, and caused an outflow of gold. This would have undermined the policy of the Treasury, which was to accumulate a gold reserve adequate for ultimate resumption.

The deflationary policy did not require an actual contraction of the currency — a measure always fraught with political danger. In fact, thanks largely to an increase in bank deposits and bank notes, the supply of money in the hands of the public grew steadily from 1870 to 1875 and again after 1878. The drastic — and to gold standard strategists satisfactory — fall in the price level came not from an actual fall in the money supply, as Greenback theorists seemed to think, but from a rapid rise in real output that outpaced the growth in the money supply. The American economy was being allowed to grow into its monetary skin. The contribution of those who controlled monetary policy was simply to resist political demands for large new issues of greenbacks. Economic growth did the rest.[8] Meanwhile, the Greenback men in their opposition to deflation fortified an illusion that the silver movement was to inherit. In focusing on greenbacks as though they were the only hope of expanding the money supply, they tended to ignore the sustained increase in the money supply that was being made available by the activities of the banks, and particularly by a large increase in demand deposits. The entire overemphasis on the monetary factor in the business cycle, and the corresponding neglect of other factors, which colored the views of both sides during the battle of the standards in the 1890's, was thus strengthened during the Greenback period.

At any rate, many men of otherwise conservative views and substantial interests were convinced during this period that the return to gold was being bought at a terrible price. But the deflationists were successful in realizing their aims: the greenbacks soon began to recover their value in relation to gold. In 1875 Congress passed the Resumption Act, providing for a return to specie payments on January 1, 1879. The greenback dollar itself steadily rose in value until it finally achieved parity

[8] On deflation and specie resumption, see James K. Kindahl, "Economic Factors in Specie Resumption in the United States, 1865–79," *Journal of Economic History*, 69 (February 1961), 30–48. On the Greenback movement, see the forthcoming comprehensive study by Irwin Unger, and in the money supply two essays by J. G. Gurley and E. S. Shaw, "The Growth of Debt and Money in the United States, 1800–1950: A Suggested Interpretation," *Review of Economics and Statistics*, 41 (August 1959), 250–262, esp. p. 258; and chapter 4 of Seymour Harris, ed., *American Economic History* (New York 1961), esp. pp. 111–114.

with gold two weeks before the date set for resumption.

Every informed person understood that when specie payments were resumed they would be made in gold alone. Here it may help to bear in mind a distinction between the legal and the factual state of the monetary standard to avoid a confusion that afflicted Harvey and some of his contemporaries. In the beginning, the United States had been legally committed to bimetallism. But in order to have a successful bimetallic standard in fact, a government must be able so to adjust the value of the two metals as to keep them both in circulation. Bimetallism implies that the government will define its monetary unit — in our case, the dollar — as having a certain weight in both metals, maintain their convertibility at a fixed ratio, freely allow their import and export, and buy or coin them in unlimited quantities when they are brought to the mint. It is easy to see how the mechanism of the bimetallic system can be thrown into disorder. The mint ratio of exchange set by the government must correspond very closely with the world market ratio which reflects demand and supply for both monetary and nonmonetary uses of the metals. If one of the two metals tends to be worth more in the market than it is at the mint, it is not likely to be brought there for coinage in material amounts.[9] It will go into industrial use or into

[9] Or at least so respectable economic theory tells us. Unfortunately the actual behavior of men in the market does not always fully correspond with the theoretical expectations. In American experience the countervailing facts were such that substantial amounts of silver were presented for coinage while gold was overvalued, and even considerable amounts of gold while silver was overvalued. See H. Gordon Hayes's monitory note, "Bimetallism Before and After 1834," *American Economic Review*, 23 (December 1933), 677–679, and the circumspect account in Neil Carothers, *Fractional Money* (New York, 1930), chapter vii. While the facts as to coinage did not adapt themselves very neatly to the requirements of economic theory, the character of the money in actual circulation did so well enough.

hoarding, leaving the other metal as the single circulating medium. Thus, if the mint ratio differs significantly from the market ratio, the two metals will circulate together only for a limited time. (Of course, if a number of governments with a sufficient combined demand can concur in a mint ratio, their joint action will tend to stabilize the value of the metals and make possible their simultaneous circulation.)

When the monetary system was organized under Hamilton's guidance, the mint ratio set by Congress at his suggestion was 15 to 1 — that is, 15 ounces of silver would exchange for one ounce of gold. But the commercial market ratio adhered fairly closely to 15.5 to 1 — a figure at which it tended to be stabilized because this was the French mint ratio. Since France valued gold more highly in relation to silver than we did, it became profitable for money brokers to export gold and import silver; after 1800 gold was in circulation only in minuscule amounts, after 1825 not at all. In effect, the nation was on silver.

In 1834, for reasons which need not detain us here, Congress intentionally pushed the pendulum too far in the opposite direction by setting the mint ratio at 16 to 1, expecting that silver would now be displaced by gold. For about a dozen years afterward the two metals circulated together, but at length silver dollars became a rarity. In 1850 the Chairman of the House Committee on Ways and Means remarked: "We have had but a single standard for the last three or four years. That has been and now is gold."[10] The coup de grâce was given to

[10] J. Laurence Laughlin, *The History of Bimetallism in the United States* (New York, 1885), pp. 78–79; see also pp. 52–74 for the background of the Act of 1834. The best informed and most perspicuous single work I have found on currency history is Neil Carothers, *Fractional Money*, which of necessity goes beyond the constricted promise of its title.

silver circulation by the mid-century discoveries of gold in California and Australia, which so lowered the value of gold in relation to silver that the silver in a silver dollar became worth about $1.03. It was now worth while to melt or export such dollars (and even fractional silver currency), for their silver content rather than to use them as money.

While still in law committed to bimetallism, the United States had thus been actually on a kind of alternating standard, resting on silver most of the time from 1792 to 1834, and soon after that year, on gold. The disappearance of silver from circulation for a generation caused most men to think of gold alone when they thought of the specie standard in the 1870's.

This fact provides the background to the Coinage Act of 1873, which within a few years of its uneventful passage was to become enormously controversial. The Act of 1873 was simply an attempt to codify the coinage practices of the country and to simplify the fractional currency which was in a chaotic state at the end of the Civil War. But in enumerating the coins that were to be maintained, the framers of the act dropped from the list the long defunct silver dollar. At that moment, the silver in a dollar was still worth $1.03,[11] and silver was not being brought to the mint for coinage in any consequential amount. Although changes were already in motion that would shortly lower the value of silver, only the most foresighted and perspicacious students of money could have foreseen that the value of silver would so soon drop

[11] While this was true of the silver dollar, it was not true of fractional silver pieces. In 1853 Congress had discovered that fractional coins could be kept in circulation, thus solving a long acute shortage of fractional money, if their silver content was reduced to a point somewhat below face value.

so much. The abandonment of the standard silver dollar, which meant the end of legal bimetallism, was not objected to by any of the representatives of silver states in Congress in 1873 nor by anyone else. But the adoption of the Coinage Act happened to coincide closely with the outbreak of a grave depression and another price collapse, and came just on the eve of a drastic fall in the world price of silver. When the Act of 1873 was followed by the Resumption Act of 1875, it was clear to everyone that in 1879, when specie payments were to be resumed, the United States would be in law as it had long been in fact on the gold standard. Now the inflationists, though still stressing the defense of the greenbacks, began to demand the remonetization of silver as a remedy for falling prices. Soon the demand for the free and unlimited coinage of silver at 16 to 1 replaced the greenback issue as the dominant platform of the cheap money men.

A glance at international price trends from the early 1870's to the middle 1890's will clarify the continuing force of the demand for monetary inflation and the prevalence of world-wide agricultural discontent. The secular downward movement of prices coincided with the formation and spread of the international gold standard, which was considered by many respectable contemporary analysts to be its primary cause. In 1871 (not in 1873, as Harvey dates it) the new German Empire gave the first of a series of shocks to silver when it resolved to adopt the gold standard, and two years afterward it threw upon the world market substantial supplies of silver realized from melting its old coins. The prospect of absorbing this much silver was too much for the countries of the Latin Union — France, Belgium, Switzerland, Italy, and Greece. In 1873 and 1874 they ceased the free and unlimited coinage of silver, thus removing from the market the primary force that had served to stabilize the value of the white metal. Sweden, Norway, and Holland also followed Germany in adopting the gold standard. These events coincided with the opening of huge new deposits of silver in the American West, which boosted silver supplies just as demand for its use as money was fast declining in the Western world. At the very time the "Coin" Harveys were sweating to extract more silver from their "Silver Bells," the price of the metal was undermined. Standing at $1.32 an ounce in 1872, it fell to $1.11 in 1884 and to 63 cents in 1894.

This fall in the price of silver, though more acute, roughly paralleled the general world price trend from the 1870's to the 1890's. In the United States, the level of prices fell sharply with each depression and rallied only slightly in good times. This price trend was a constant hazard to certain types of new and marginal entrepreneurs, dependent on easy credit and especially vulnerable to business shocks; but of course it struck with particular severity those chronic debtors, the farmers. Above all, it was intolerable to those farmers who were producing a large portion of their crops for export into a world market increasingly oversupplied with their products — the growers of wheat and cotton. The swiftness and fatality of the fall in the prices of these two agricultural products outstripped all others. Wheat, which brought $1.37 a bushel in 1870, was down to 56 cents in 1894; raw cotton in the same years went from 23 cents a pound to seven cents. It is easy to see why Coin, hoping to demonstrate the community of interests of farmers and silver, should have chosen to exhibit a table (p. 200) comparing the price histories of just three products: silver, cotton, and wheat. It is a defensible oversimplification to say that the inflationary movement in politics rested mainly upon the common concern of these three segments of the economy, each confronted with a disastrous oversupply of its product in the world market.

V

When the free silver men won control of the inflationary forces, they inherited from the Greenbackers a formidable body of agitational literature and political folklore. The Greenback movement had succeeded in focusing the vanguard dissenting mind on monetary policy as the primary solution of the nation's ills; and in its opposition to bond issues and gold accumulation as the basis for currency contraction, it had already convinced many people that they were being victimized by a bondholders' conspiracy and that the issue of bonds for sale in foreign markets reduced them to "'hewers of wood and drawers of water' to foreigners." To convert this heritage of agitation to its own uses, the silver movement had to overcome the prejudice held by fiat money men against all forms of specie, including silver.[12]

But as against the Greenbackers, the silver men had some advantages. The first was intellectual: fiat money seemed unlimited and arbitrary, but hard silver money

[12] In its first national platform of 1876 the Greenback party mentioned silver only to protest against the replacement of paper fractional currency by silver coins as a policy which, "although well calculated to enrich owners of silver mines . . . will still further oppress in taxation an already overburdened people." By 1880 its platform called for "the unlimited coinage of silver as well as gold." In 1884 its platform boasted: "We forced the remonetization of the silver dollar," referring presumably to the Bland-Allison Act. K. H. Porter and D. B. Johnson, *National Party Platforms* (Urbana, Ill., 1956), pp. 52, 57, 68.

was tied to a metal of limited supply, of long historic sanction among the money systems of the world, and supported by great economists and statesmen. Legal bimetallism had been traditional in the United States as well as in many other parts of the world; silver could be called, with some oversimplification, "the dollar of our daddies," the staple of the currency system from Washington and Jefferson to Jackson. The second advantage was political: the silver-producing states had a formidable bloc in Congress; silver had a good following in both major parties — in sharp contrast with the Greenback party, which even at its height in 1878 did not elect a single Senator. The silver states, backed by their allies from the wheat and cotton states, could not easily be ignored. The final advantage was financial: silver mining interests were able to bring to the silver movement more financial backing than the Greenback movement ever had. As time went on, the paper money commitment of the Greenback tradition faded into the background, while its more adaptable sentiments about the world, its hostilities to bankers, bondholders, foreigners and monopolists, were taken over by the silver spokesmen.

In 1878 the silver men had their first legislative success. Discontents aroused during the years of depression since 1873 had led to a great increase in silver agitation in all sections of the country from Pennsylvania to California, and many manufacturers joined with the silver and agrarian inflationists. Late in 1877 the House passed a bill introduced by "Silver Dick" Bland of Missouri calling for free coinage of silver and full legal tender. The margin was overwhelming: 163 to 34. Secretary of the Treasury John Sherman, still preoccupied with the success of his measures for refunding and resumption, saw that some compromises would have to be made with the forces opposed to monetary contraction. Fortified by the knowledge that free coinage would be blocked by the certain veto of President Hayes, he was able to rally Senate opposition around a compromise finally embodied in the Bland-Allison Act of 1878. This measure required the Secretary of the Treasury to buy and to have coined into dollars having full legal tender not less than $2,000,000 nor more than $4,000,000 worth of silver bullion each month. Although he strongly opposed the legal tender provision, Sherman resigned himself to accepting it: "In a government like ours, it is always good to obey the popular current, and that has been done, I think, by the passage of the silver bill." [13] Happily the passage of this measure coincided with the return of prosperity, but it stemmed neither the general price decline nor the fall in the price of silver. Although conservative secretaries of the Treasury consistently bought the minimum required amounts of silver, over $378,000,000 were issued under the provisions of the law, chiefly in the form of silver certificates.

The demand for silver purchases only increased with the agricultural crisis of the late 1880's. In 1889–90 the silver bloc in Congress received powerful reinforcements when six new Western states committed to silver entered the Union. In 1890, to win needed support for its high-tariff program, the Harrison administration made a new concession to the silver men by stepping up the level of silver purchases. The Sherman Silver Purchase Act of 1890 required the Secretary of the Treasury to buy 4,500,000 ounces of silver each month — an amount equal to

[13] Jeannette P. Nichols, "John Sherman and the Silver Drive of 1877–78: The Origins of the Gigantic Subsidy," *Ohio Archaeological and Historical Quarterly*, 46 (April 1937), 164; this article provides the most circumstantial account of this compromise.

the approximate output of domestic silver mines — and again to issue legal tender Treasury notes in payment for it.

The existence of so large an amount of silver certificates was a threat to the gold reserves of the Treasury which had been so carefully built up by Sherman and his predecessors. Under the Sherman Act, the Secretary of the Treasury was required to maintain the two metals "at a parity," which meant that the silver certificates were to be as good as gold. The government was now committed to keep at par with gold all the old greenbacks still remaining in circulation and the silver dollars and the Treasury notes of 1890. Since the Treasury was required to redeem these obligations in gold, they represented a potential demand against its gold supply. The capacity of the Treasury to stand the strain depended on conditions of general prosperity. Prosperity brought about a substantial Treasury surplus, which left a comfortable margin for the luxury of silver purchases. The gold reserve was also momentarily strengthened by years of big European demand for American crops in 1879–1881 and in 1891, which brought inflows of gold.

But even before the crisis of 1893, the Harrison administration had begun to undermine the surplus. Tariff revenues, then the main source of government funds, were cut by some provisions of the tariff of 1890, while an extravagant pension act and other enlarged expenditures made big new demands on federal funds. A growing anxiety in the business community about the state of the Treasury's gold stocks sent gold into hoarding. To meet its expenses the Treasury found that it had to pay out greenbacks and Treasury notes, but as these were soon presented for gold redemption they constituted a potential endless drain on gold supplies. When the central banks of European countries, themselves afflicted by depression and shaken by the failure of the House of Baring in 1890, began to tighten their gold policies, the situation grew worse.

Many years before, $100,000,000 in gold had been set aside as the Treasury reserve deemed necessary to assure successful resumption. In time this figure, considered to be the level of a safe Treasury reserve, came to have a kind of magic significance among right-thinking men in the financial community. As Grover Cleveland put it, the figure was regarded "with a sort of sentimental solicitude." Only six weeks after his inauguration in 1893, the gold reserve fell below this figure, and soon afterward there began a headlong financial panic, marked by a stock market collapse and a run on banks throughout the country. Cleveland was also aware that India was about to close its mints to silver coinage, which would deal another staggering blow to the price of silver. It was no longer possible to pretend that the United States could afford to redeem its silver issues in gold and stay on the gold standard. Accepting the necessity for a showdown with the silver forces, Cleveland called on June 30 for a special session of Congress to repeal the Sherman Silver Purchase Act.

The prosperity that had made it possible to compromise between silver inflationism and the gold standard was now gone, and in consequence the ensuing Congressional debate had all the bitterness that occurs when no real accommodation of interests is possible. The gold men attributed the panic almost entirely to the silver purchase policy and to the failure of business confidence that had been created by uncertainty about future values and by threats to foreign trade and investments. They expatiated on the folly of a commitment to silver at a time when the metal was constantly falling in value and when its use as standard money had been abandoned by all the great trading nations of the West.

Silver men saw the panic in quite different terms: again and again they charged that it had been deliberately set off by heartless bankers simply to create conditions of distress under which they could force the repeal of the Sherman Act.[14] As for the Sherman Act itself, they held no brief for it, since what was really needed was the free and unlimited coinage of silver. But they saw it as the line of defense of the silver cause — "the last feeble barrier," a Populist Senator from Nebraska called it, "between the patriotic and industrious masses of our people and that hoard of insolent, aggressive, and ravenous money-changers and gamblers of Lombard street and Wall street, who for private gain would . . . turn the world back into the gloom of the Dark Ages with all its attendant evil and misery." [15] When they were told that it was utterly impossible for the United States acting alone to maintain a parity between the two metals and that unlimited coinage was unthinkable at the existing ratio, they tended to fall back upon assertions of the size and grandeur of the United States, aspersions upon the states of Europe, and reminders of the pitiful economic condition of their constituents. In answer to the argument that free coinage would in effect mean silver monometallism, they might assert, as Senator Cockrell

[14] Though most of them were ready to admit that the panic had got out of hand. Cf. "Silver Dick" Bland: "Now the panic has come; and those who conspired to bring it about have got more than they bargained for." William V. Byars, *An American Commoner* (Columbia, Mo., 1900), p. 330; cf, the view of Senator Teller of Colorado, in Elmer Ellis, *Henry Moore Teller* (Caldwell, Idaho, 1941), pp. 222–223.

[15] Senator William V. Allen, *Congressional Record*, 53rd Congress, 1st sess., pp. 788–789 (August 24, 1893).

of Missouri later did, that this would be so much the better: "They can't exhaust the gold reserves too quickly to suit me. We can go to a silver basis without as much as a ripple in our financial system." [16]

Among those prominent in the Congressional debates was William Jennings Bryan, who made a long and stirring speech in the House. In the Senate, where action was delayed by an exhausting filibuster, the silver case was argued by some of its ablest exponents, notably Senator Teller of Colorado, who, in the course of describing the miseries that would befall his own state if repeal passed, broke down in tears, slumped to his desk, and buried his face in his hands. Nothing availed: repeal was finally enacted at the end of October 1893, and the silver men had to rest their hopes on an appeal to the public.[17]

It was here that Harvey found his role. All these climactic events must have absorbed his attention during the eighteen months before the appearance of his book. He moved to Chicago precisely at the outbreak of the panic, and was busy setting up the Coin Publishing Company during the months when the silver debate was nearing its climax. His first publication, a book by Archbishop Walsh of Dublin on *Bimetallism and Monometallism*, appeared two months after the Congressional decision on repeal. Although he had shown some interest in bimetallism a few years before, no one knows precisely what silver arguments, beyond Walsh's, he had read.[18] But

[16] Barnes, *Carlisle*, p. 367.

[17] On the fight over repeal see Allan Nevins, *Grover Cleveland* (New York, 1932), chapter xxix; and Jeannette P. Nichols, "The Politics and Personalities of Silver Repeal in the United States Senate," *American Historical Review*, 41 (October 1935), 26–53.

[18] Harvey's essay, "The Free-Silver Argument," *Forum*, 19 (June 1895), 401–409, recapitulates the main argument of his book, and documents it with collections of statutes and statistics, as well as the Reports of the Monetary Commissions of 1876 and 1878.

if he had read even a small part of the hundreds of pages of speeches in the *Congressional Record* taken up by the debate over repeal, he could have found there a basis for all but the most idiosyncratic of his economic arguments for silver, and he could have found confirmation of all his underlying attitudes and convictions.

vi

No doubt the wide currency of these attitudes, which gave the book its rapport with ordinary readers, had as much to do with the success of *Coin's Financial School* as its central economic exposition. Before going on to Harvey's notions about finance, it will be profitable to listen to the tonalities of his work.

Young Coin himself is a suggestive symbol. Though he tackles the most intricate of subjects and offers to solve the most perplexing problems, Coin is not a wise old man but a figure of youth, almost of childhood. He is drawn by Harvey's cartoonist as dressed in tails and carrying a top hat, but his pants are knee breeches, his face is boyish, and he is referred to as "the young financier," and "the little lecturer." In a subsequent book Harvey seemed to push Coin's age back even further by remarking that Coin was only ten years old at the time of these lectures. The choice of such a figure as his spokesman implied that the intricacies of economics, once the distracting features of selfishness and self-delusion were set aside, were not too great to be mastered by the acute, simple, and unspoiled mind of a boy, and hence that the intuitions of the common man about the money question were sounder than the complex sophistries of bankers and hireling professors of economics.[19] Harvey took

[19] As Congressman Edward Lane of Illinois said during the House debates on the repeal of the Sherman Silver Purchase Act, "Mr.

as a congenial Biblical text for the volume Matthew 11:25: "I thank thee, O Father, Lord of Heaven and Earth, because thou hast hid these things from the wise and prudent, and hast revealed them unto babes."

Throughout Harvey's writings the notion recurs that the old are thoroughly corrupted by selfishness and that the hope of civilization lies in setting youth on the straight path. The school conducted by Coin at the Art Institute is established in the first instance for the youth of Chicago, in the hope that they may be led "out of the labyrinth of falsehoods, heresies, and isms that distract the country." It is only after Coin's first lecture succeeds brilliantly with the young that he is requested to open his school to men of all ages, whereupon it is promptly packed with "middle-aged and old men" who hope to confound the youngster with "knotty questions." Now the big businessmen of Chicago get their come-uppance: it is they, and not Coin, who are befuddled. "They had listened critically, expecting to detect errors in his facts or reasoning. There were none. They were amazed. He was logical . . . That it should come from the lips of a boy they were more surprised." "Coin was like a little monitor in the midst of a fleet of wooden ships. His shots went through and silenced all opposition." The mastery of innocent but well-schooled youth over guileful age is complete. The fathers, by their inept conduct of affairs, had brought the country to the edge of disaster. Coin spoke for the hope that lay in the sons.

Harvey portrayed the departure from bimetallism as

Speaker, my people do not have to consult Chevalier, John Stuart Mill, Ricardo, or any other writer on finance in order to understand their conditions. They know from personal knowledge that they occupy the garden spot of this whole rich country; that their crops for the last decade have been reasonably abundant, yet their pocketbooks are empty." Barnes, *Carlisle*, p. 268.

a kind of violation of natural order, a willful failure to make use of the *two* metals God had put at man's disposal for use as money, and hence as a kind of disobedience to divine will. "As the two legs are necessary to walk and two eyes to see, so were these two monies necessary to the prosperity of the people." But though both are necessary, they do not have an equal moral or economic significance. Silver, which had historically been the base or component of such small currency units as the ordinary man was likely to see or handle, was held to be the money of the people. Gold was the money of the rich. Silver, which had been abundant, was identified with plenty, gold with niggardliness. The metals were given human characters and fates: poor downtrodden silver was shut out of the mints, while gold, the pampered and petted, was welcomed in. This anthropomorphic treatment of the metals, one of which stood for the downtrodden and neglected masses of farmers and honest working people was carried out in the cartoons, and found its way into Harvey's language when he spoke of the Act of 1873 as having "deprived silver of its *right* to unrestricted coinage."

Popular suspicion in the West and South against the East, and in rural areas against the city, and in folkish tradition against Britain and the monetary power of John Bull and the House of Rothschild runs through the book and is effectively caught in its cartoons. The United States is seen as having been trapped in "a financial system forced upon us by Europe." This the bankers of the great metropolitan centers accept, but it is destructive almost everywhere else. The mentality of the great centers, preoccupied with personal gain, is narrow and self-deluding. "Cities do not breed statesmen. They breed the specialist. A specialist favors what will tend to promote his business though it may injure the business of others. A statesman must be broad. He must have a comprehensive appreciation of the interests of all the people — especially the poorer classes."

The cartoons, drawn for the book by H. L. Godall or borrowed from silver newspapers, reduce these feelings to simple and striking images: gold smiles cruelly at the corpse of silver, assassinated by the pen; the West and the South, duped by the financial traps of East, finally unite to overthrow East; a cow, feeding in the West, is milked in New York (this was one of the most common of the Populist images); an octopus representing the Rothschilds, centered in England, and labelled "The Great English Devil Fish" grips the entire world in its tentacles; John Bull makes a brutal attack on the female figure of Liberty, while virtuous Silver, helpless in chains, looks on; the British lion is blown out of a cannon by the figure of Uncle Sam; an incredibly rapacious usurer sits clutching his bags of gold.

Yet for all this, Harvey's language is fairly restrained when he discusses the gold advocates. Harvey made quite a point of the idea that the abuse heaped by the conservative press on silverites was a poor substitute for rational argument, and he preferred to picture Coin as rising nobly above all this. It was, for him, a rare *ad hominem* attack when he described J. Laurence Laughlin as a "professor in a chair of political economy, endowed with the money of bankers, his mental faculties . . . trained with his salary." For the most part, Harvey preferred to picture substantial businessmen as potential friends of silver, willing to listen to reason. The bankers themselves, he said, "as a rule are a patriotic class of men, but they are controlled by a central influence in London and New York."

The stance of rationality and fair play which Harvey struck with most of his contemporaries was possible because silverite hostilities were directed elsewhere — projected backward in time, to the perpetrators of the monstrous Crime of '73, and outward in space, to Britain as the bulwark of the international gold standard and to the House of Rothschild as its financial center. When Harvey discusses the Crime of '73 and the power of Britain, his claim breaks down. The alleged disaster of the demonetization of silver in 1873 was not viewed by Harvey, or by most silverites, as the consequence of a ghastly mistake but as the outcome of a crafty conspiracy. Demonetization, the work of "men having a design to injure business by making money scarce," had accomplished exactly what had been intended: it had created a depression and caused untold suffering. The law of 1873 was passed stealthily, and many of the men who voted for it had no notion of what they were doing. Silver was "demonetized secretly, and since then a powerful money trust has used deception and misrepresentations that have led thousands of honest minds astray." Demonetization

is commonly known as the crime of 1873. A crime, because it has confiscated millions of dollars worth of property. A crime, because it has made thousands of paupers. A crime, because it has made tens of thousands of tramps. A crime, because it has made thousands of suicides. A crime, because it has brought tears to strong men's eyes, and hunger and pinching want to widows and orphans. A crime, because it is destroying the honest yeomanry of the land, the bulwark of the nation. A crime, because it has brought this once great republic to the verge of ruin, where it is now in imminent danger of tottering to its fall. [Applause.]

The true center of this criminal conspiracy is, of course, London. Almost every step in Coin's argument is interlarded with a renewal of the old hostility to England, and there are times when one feels that one is back in the atmosphere of 1812. Even the foundations of our monetary system, it is argued, dated from "our revolutionary forefathers, who had a hatred of England, and an intimate knowledge of her designs on this country." Harvey had an important tactical reason for wanting to exploit this feeling. The advocates of unilateral free coinage of silver by the United States were carrying on an argument not only with gold standard advocates but with the international bimetallists, who believed that the use of both metals in monetary standards was desirable but insisted that the United States could not uphold silver unaided without disaster. The argument of the international bimetallists was in fact one of the most formidable arguments of the opponents of unilateral free silver, and a certain frustration in dealing with it no doubt had something to do with the violent rhetoric in which Harvey put his case.

The climactic passage of *Coin's Financial School* occurs in Coin's sixth and last lecture, in which he spells out defiance to English power. Here he urges that the experiment of monetary independence be tried, and that if the argument of the internationalists should prove correct, one should not capitulate to gold but wage war: "If it is true, let us attach England to the United States and blot out her name from among the nations of the earth. [Applause.]" Coin goes on to say that "a war with England would be the most popular ever waged on the face of the earth," and also the most just, since it would be waged against a power that "can dictate the money of the world, and thereby create world-wide misery." But such a war, he continued, was in fact not necessary if England were defied in American monetary policy. To hope for her concurrence in international action was futile: she was a creditor nation committed to gold. "Wherever property interests and humanity have come in conflict, England has ever been the enemy of human liberty." To shirk the struggle for unilateral bimetallism "means a surrender to England" and involves the risk that internecine war will arise in the United States that will put an end to the republic. If the present policy is continued, he argued, it will end

> in England owning us body and soul. She is making a peaceable conquest of the United States. What she failed to do with shot and shell in the eighteenth century, she is doing with the gold standard in the nineteenth century. [Applause.] The conservative monied interest furnished the tory friends of England then, and it furnishes her friends now. [Applause.] The business men of New York City passed strong resolutions against the Declaration of Independence in 1776, and they are passing strong resolutions against an American policy now. [Applause]

vii

While Harvey's was unquestionably the most popular statement of the case for silver, it was far from the best. Indeed it was so much inferior to the speeches of such Congressional advocates as Bryan and Teller and to the writings of such American bimetallists as President E. Benjamin Andrews of Brown, President Francis A. Walker of M.I.T., or the silver diplomat and propagandist S. Dana Horton that one is tempted to propound a Gresham's law of popular monetary discussion, by which the weak arguments drive the strong out of circulation. Harvey's case is not developed systematically or logically, and his sense for what is important among the issues is almost touchingly unsure. His greatest failing was his staggering gift for irrelevancy — his readiness to inject into the argument assertions that were either unnecessary to his case or incapable of substantiation. He attached, for example, the highest importance to his assertion that all the gold in the world could be incorporated into a cube of 22 feet; he portrayed Coin's goldbug auditors as being thrown almost into paroxysms by this revelation, although no one was disposed to deny that gold was a scarce commodity. He tempted the ridicule of economists by insisting that it cost $2.00 an ounce to produce silver, when silver had not brought a price of more than about $1.36 an ounce within the memory of living man — thus implying that the metal had been produced for more than a generation out of philanthropy. He made errors of fact, he distorted statutes and quotations, he invented his own confusing terminology ("redemption money"), he forced side issues or nonissues into the center of attention, he made up a monetary history that was largely fictional, and, all in all, made himself vastly more vulnerable to his critics than his case required.[20]

Indeed, almost everything about Harvey's book can be argued with except its success. The importance of Harvey's pamphlet for the student of history lies in its popularity, which suggests that Harvey's understanding of the case was close to that held by the ordinary silverite of firm convictions and active intelligence but no special training. Harvey was what Gertrude Stein once called another money crank, Ezra Pound — "a village explain-

[20] The most important contemporary critiques, which go at Harvey's argument point by point, are J. Laurence Laughlin's *Facts about Money* (Chicago, 1895), and Horace White's *Coin's Financial Fool* (New York, 1895). Willard Fisher's article, " 'Coin' and his Critics," already cited, made a scrupulous effort to defend Harvey, ("an untrained thinker of considerably more than average ability") at a few points where Fisher felt that Harvey's critics had done him injustice, but also marshals (pp. 190–192) a brief list of Harvey's most extraordinary and gratuitous errors.

er." Like many another movement, free silver had its lowbrow and highbrow culture. Harvey represents the common man thinking, and the essentials of his argument reproduce a very widespread contemporary view. These essentials may be extracted from his cluttered exposition. They consist of four assertions that are primarily historical in character and four that are primarily programmatic and economic. The historical assertions are that the original unit of American currency was the silver dollar, adopted in 1792; that this was the primary element of a successful bimetallic system down to 1873; that in 1873 silver was "secretly" and stealthily demonetized by a Congress so hypnotized or so corrupted by sinister gold interests that it did not know what it was doing; and that the demonetization of silver in 1873 deprived the country of half the supply of its primary money. The assertions that might be regarded as largely economic are that the depression and misery which the country had endured were simply the consequences of falling prices and the continuing appreciation of gold; that low prices could be remedied by an infusion of new money; that the appropriate source of new money was free and unlimited coinage of silver at 16 to 1; and finally, that this remedy could be successfully adopted by the United States acting alone and without the cooperation of any foreign country.

Harvey's history of the original American currency system was in fact completely irrelevant to the merits of free coinage of silver as a remedy for the economic conditions of the 1890's. If free silver was good policy in 1894, it mattered not in the least what coinage the Founding Fathers had intended in 1792. After a hundred years of additional experience with currency systems and some advance in economic knowledge, one could hardly expect the currency practices of the founders to have much rational authority for Harvey's contemporaries on either side of the currency issue. But the silver men, like their opponents, cherished their historical lore, and the happy notion that free coinage of silver would restore "the dollar of our daddies" was an important part of it.

Harvey's version of the history of American money could hardly have been more misleading. His elaborate attempt to establish that the original monetary unit was a *silver* dollar, and that gold was "also made money" but that "its value was counted from the silver dollar" is nonsensical, as well as gratuitous. The original monetary unit was simply the dollar, circulated in a variety of pieces of both gold and silver.[21] The dollar was defined as having a certain weight of silver and a certain weight of gold, bearing to each other the proportions of 15 to 1. The fathers did not in fact cherish any preference for silver over gold. Gold was widely preferred as having a more certain and stable value; but Hamilton, in his report on coinage to Congress in May, 1791, recommended a bimetallic unit on the ground that the available quantity of gold was not sufficient to serve as the basis for a money system. If one tries to salvage whatever there may be of fact in Harvey's attempt to claim primacy for silver, it must be simply that gold, being too valuable to serve as common coin, was coined only in units ranging from $2.50 up to the $10 gold eagle, and that the coinage handled by the common man was of silver. ("Gold was considered the money of the rich . . . the poor people seldom handled it, and the very poor people seldom ever saw any of it.")

Harvey's implication that the United States had a

[21] The coinage measure of 1792 provided for three gold coins worth $10, $5, and $2.50, for a silver dollar, and for silver half dollars, quarters, dimes and half dimes, as well as a copper penny and half penny.

smoothly working bimetallic system before the "Crime of 73" and that the old American silver dollar had wide circulation in this country was also misleading. In law, as we have seen, bimetallism did exist. In fact, the standard had alternated from silver to gold because Congress failed to set a mint ratio in accord with the world market. This very alternation of standards later persuaded dogmatic gold men to insist — all too glibly — that bimetallism had been proved to be an impossibility. They failed to take into account the fact that it would not have been impossible to arrive at a mint ratio more in harmony with France's, if the will to do it had been present in Congress at any time between the days of Hamilton and the Civil War. It is tempting to speculate how much strength international bimetallism might have acquired, if Congress had decided soon after 1792 to rectify Hamilton's miscalculation and establish a common ratio with France.

As for the old American silver dollar, Harvey seemed unaware that it had disappeared rapidly from circulation not long after Congress provided for its coinage. This came about because the standard American silver dollar, though lighter in weight than the Spanish silver dollar, was newer, brighter, and less abraded, and thus became more acceptable in certain kinds of foreign trade. Dealers found it profitable to export it in exchange for the Spanish dollars, which were legal tender in the United States, and which became our primary medium of silver circulation. As a consequence of the drainage of the American silver dollar, President Jefferson ordered its coinage discontinued in 1806, and this suspension remained in force for thirty years.

The third of Harvey's historical assertions — that the Coinage Act of 1873 was passed in secret corruption at the instance of the gold bankers — was a point of faith among money agitators and had been widely believed for sixteen years. Despite its intrinsic implausibility, gold spokesmen were forced to make elaborate refutations of this charge. No measure could pass Congress in secret, they pointed out, and the Coinage Act had been before Congress almost three years from April 1870 to its passage in February 1873; the Chairman of the House Committee of Coinage, Weights and Measures, introducing it to the House, pointed to its establishment of legal monometallism and declared that it had come to him from a Senate Committee that had given it "as careful attention as I have ever known a committee to bestow on any measure"; it was printed thirteen times by order of Congress; it had been debated once in the Senate and twice in the House for a total of 144 columns of the *Congressional Globe*; two Directors of the Mint and other experts had pointed out that the bill demonetized the old silver dollar; Samuel Hooper of Massachusetts, who steered the bill through the House, carefully observed that the gold dollar was being established as the standard of value; several senators referred to the cessation of coinage of the silver dollar; and some of the quotations silver men later invoked to show the stealthy passage of the bill were arrived at by misrepresenting Congressional debates.[22]

However, when a delusion like that of the "Crime of '73" get to be so widely believed, it is perhaps quite as

[22] For standard refutations by gold advocates, see Laughlin, *Facts about Money*, pp. 57–69 and *The History of Bimetallism*, pp. 95–102; Horace White, *Coin's Financial Fool*, pp. 44–54; David K. Watson, *History of American Coinage* (New York, 1899), pp. 125–137. By far the most knowledgeable and astute account of the origins of the law of 1873 that I have found is Neil Carothers, *Fractional Money*, chapter xvi, and my estimate of the situation follows his.

important to understand how it came about as to repeat elaborate proofs of its falsity. No doubt economic suffering and social resentments had a great deal to do with the formation and spread of the myth. But there was a soupçon of truth out of which the notion of the Crime of '73 grew: it lies in the fact that even the better-informed men in Congress could hardly have had a very keen sense in 1873 of the full implications of what they were doing when they passed the Coinage Act.

This measure was intended in the first instance to codify the coinage laws and to remedy the chaotic and expensive condition in which our fractional currency had been left at the end of the Civil War. After much talk of the need of such action in the late 1860's, John Jay Knox, the Deputy Comptroller of the Currency, was requested by Secretary of the Treasury George Boutwell to prepare such a bill. It was first presented to Congress in 1870, and was much discussed and amended in the three years before its passage. The question of providing for continued coinage of the standard silver dollar was never an issue, and no attentive Congressman need have had difficulty in understanding that its coinage was being dropped. The silver dollar, exported before 1806, not coined from 1806 to 1836, and not circulated from 1836 to 1873, was simply an unfamiliar and half-forgotten coin. No one objected to its discontinuance, not because there was any secret about the matter, but because no one cared. The silver interests, who knew that the weight of silver specified for the defunct silver dollar was actually worth a few cents more than a dollar in the open market, had no reason to demand its continued coinage. When the law of 1873 was introduced, Germany had not yet gone on the gold standard, and even when it was passed the effect of German silver sales in the world market had not yet begun to depress the price of the metal.

Seven months after the passage of the Coinage Act the panic of 1873 began, and the fall in the price of silver began at about the same time. It was natural for money-oriented reformers to connect the two events. As inflationary demands built up, Congressmen who found it politic to take up a prosilver position now began to explain that in voting for the Coinage Act of 1873 they had not known what they were doing — and if one bears in mind the technical character of the law, it becomes evident that in a certain sense most of them were telling the truth. But for at least a few of them, to join in the general cry about the "Crime of '73" required a certain daring mendacity. For example, Representative William D. Kelley of Pennsylvania, the same man who is quoted above as having assured the House how carefully the bill had been weighed in committee, was one of the few who explicitly pointed out the implications of the Coinage Act for silver. He told the House on January 9, 1872: "It is impossible to retain the double standard." Yet six years later Kelley brazenly joined those who insisted that the Coinage Act of 1873 was a fraud, when he said that, "though the chairman of the committee on coinage, I was ignorant of the fact that it would demonetize the silver dollar, or of its dropping the silver dollar from our system of coins."

As for Harvey's contention that the Act of 1873, by demonetizing silver, "destroyed one-half of the redemption money of the United States," his critics were fond of pointing out that a kind of money that was not in circulation at all could hardly have been destroyed, and that it could not conceivably have had any consequences for the depression of 1873–1879, since the country was then still on the inconvertible paper standard. They were also fond of pointing out that by the silver acts of 1878 and 1890 silver dollars had in some measure been restored to circulation. In fact more silver dollars or silver certificates having legal tender status had been put in circulation by 1894 than anyone could have dreamed of in 1873 — without having lifted the general price level or the price of silver itself.[23]

The history of our money is full of its own subtle mockeries, and there is one ironic aspect of the law of 1873 that must be noted here: far from having demonetized silver in any operative sense, it actually came close to remonetizing the white metal, despite the intention of its framers. While the old standard silver dollar was dropped from coinage, the law created — largely to facilitate trade with the silver-standard countries of the Orient and to compete with the Mexican dollar — a new silver dollar called the trade dollar. The trade dollar had a silver content slightly greater than the old standard silver dollar and was not expected to circulate within the United States. However, the law provided that the trade dollar was not only to be freely coined but also to be legal tender for payments up to the amount of five dollars within the country. The legal tender provision was included to bolster the foreign standing of this dollar by enhancing its domestic standing. No one thought this dollar would have any actual domestic circulation, because it was at an even greater premium as silver than the lighter standard dollar that had disappeared, and it was not expected to compete for circulation with the then prevailing greenbacks. But the ensuing sudden drop in the value of silver and the rise in that of the greenbacks

[23] By 1894 there were in circulation $326.9 million in silver certificates, $134.6 million in Treasury notes of 1890, and $52.5 million in silver dollars. *Historical Statistics of the United States*, p. 648.

had the effect of causing the trade dollars to circulate in substantial amounts in this country, as well as being exported to the Orient. Accordingly, the legal tender character of the trade dollar was removed by Congress in 1876, and when its circulation persisted, its coinage was discontinued in 1878. Its circulation continued until it was finally redeemed by Congress in 1887. But as Charles R. Whittlesey has observed, the combined provisions for free coinage and legal tender, while they lasted, had the effect of briefly remonetizing silver; and when one takes account of the greater weight of the trade dollar, of remonetizing it at a ratio of about 16⅓ to 1—a ratio which was by no means unfavorable to silver when one considers what was happening to silver prices. But the inflationary forces, failing to see what they had inadvertently gained for their metal by the creation of the trade dollar, showed no great interest in blocking the repeal of its legal tender power. This may be attributed to their failure to understand its potentialities for remonetization. It would have been far easier, politically, to mobilize the growing silver sentiment against this repeal in 1876 than to regain free coinage of the standard silver dollar. Professor Whittlesey attributes this tactical oversight to "economic illiteracy on the part of the silver interests." [24] But on the whole one is impressed by the sense that all those involved with currency problems in the 1870's were like men groping in the dark.

viii

Let us turn now to the programmatic, as opposed to the historical, side of Harvey's argument. There are two possible ways of looking at the subject. The first is to

[24] *Principles and Practices of Money and Banking* (New York, 1954), pp. 206–208. On the trade dollar see Carothers, *Fractional Money*, pp. 233–34, 275–280. In a sense, it is almost anachronistic to

regard Harvey as though he were a professional economist, and to apply to his exposition the same rigorous standards that one would apply to any professional work. In this there is now little point, except by way of establishing the difference between popular agitation and professional analysis. Harvey was an amateur, and his book was at best a caricature of sophisticated bimetallist thought. Of course it suited contemporary defenders of the gold standard to treat him as though he were a professional, and on this ground they were for the most part unanswerable. He had, after all, presented "Coin" as an expert more authoritative than the experts. J. Laurence Laughlin perhaps spoke with too much personal asperity and failed to reckon with Harvey's honest naivete when he charged that "the book was intentionally constructed to fit into prevailing prejudices and consciously deceive," but one must bow to the more dispassionate verdict of another contemporary economist, Willard Fisher, that it was "of no value to those who have been trained to think about monetary problems," and who found it strange "that so crude a product could have created so great a sensation." [25]

But it is also possible to say that complicated issues like money do on occasion have to be made the object of popular discussion in a democracy, and that they must of necessity be discussed in a simplified way. One may then ask whether, disregarding technicalities, there was any substantive economic merit in the demand for inflation as a remedy for the depression of the nineties,

---

speak of the "silver interests" as an organized force in 1876. Sentiment for silver was just crystallizing, and the dominant inflationary rationale was still that of the Greenbackers.

[25] Laughlin, "'Coin's' Food for the Gullible," *Forum*, 19 (July 1895), p. 577; Fisher, "'Coin' and his Critics," p. 192.

and whether the demand for cheaper money did not also have some moral justification. If the issue is looked at in these broad and indulgent terms, Harvey becomes far more defensible — and in a certain way even prophetic, for in some fields of inquiry yesterday's crank may turn out to be closer than yesterday's accepted spokesman to today's dominant views.

The essence of Harvey's programmatic position is summed up on page 175, where he advocates the remonetization of silver in these words: "You increase the value of all property by adding to the number of money units in the land. You make it possible for the debtor to pay his debts; business to start anew, and revivify all the industries of the country, which must remain paralyzed so long as silver as well as all other property is measured by a gold standard." The imprecision of his way of putting things becomes apparent not only in the unintelligible though charmingly illustrated conception of business depressions that follows page 147 but also in the assertion on page 203 that cutting the gold dollar in half would "thereby double the value [presumably he meant prices] of all property in the United States, except debts." [26]

[26] Such proposals were so commonly regarded by contemporary conservatives as a form of lunatic radicalism that it is worthwhile to notice the element of latent conservatism in this overwhelming emphasis on the monetary factor in depressions. Harvey and his fellow silverites were not trying to develop a fundamental critique of industrial capitalism; they were merely trying to make it work, and they believed that the device that would do so was essentially a simple one. This premise went unnoticed by their conservative critics, but not by the left wing of the Populist party, whose spokesmen objected to free silver on the ground, among others, that it would not go very far to alleviate the basic ills of American society.

It is perhaps important to point out that in 1933, when the gold content of the dollar was cut to 59 per cent of its previous parity, in the hope of bringing about a proportionate rise in prices, the expedient did not work.

Harvey was, of course, using a rudimentary version of the quantity theory of money. Given stable conditions of demand for money, its value will vary inversely with the quantity available. Hence the general price level varies directly with this quantity. A massive addition to the money supply such as that promised by free coinage of silver would raise the general price level, return inflated debts to a fair level, and reinvigorate the entire economy.

There is a certain danger that we may become so absorbed in the inadequacies of Harvey's case for inflation, and in particular of the quixotic case for free coinage of silver at 16 to 1, that we will ignore the substantial merits of the demand for inflation. Modern economic opinion would treat Harvey's general line of reasoning, especially as applied to the depression of the 1890's which came after a long period of drastic deflation, with much greater respect than dogmatic contemporary professionals. What vitiated Harvey's point of view was his obsession with the bullion basis of the money supply, which in turn reflects his adherence to an old-fashioned view of money, inherited from American agrarian thought. He did not think of money functionally, as a means of payment, but simply as money of account (or, as he would say, a measure of value). He understood "true" money to consist in hard coin. The quantity theory of money, as he employed it (page 188), applied only to "redemption money" — that is, gold or silver. The elaborate apparatus of credit that was growing up in his lifetime he dismissed as irrelevant to the fundamental issue of the monetary standard. The expansion of what he called "credit money" represented no real addition to the money supply — and its overexpansion he could regard only as dangerous (pages 141–143).

Modern statements of the quantity theory of money

measure the money supply by taking into account all the means of payment that are available, including demand deposits — i.e., bank deposits subject to withdrawal by check. They also consider the velocity of monetary circulation as a dimension that must be taken into account when the supply of money is estimated for any period of time. The concept of velocity, though an old one, was just beginning to be employed in empirical study in Harvey's time; but the fast growing use of demand deposits was a familiar and measurable fact to his contemporaries. By the 1890's something like 90% of the volume of business transactions was being carried on by check. Harvey could not be persuaded to take any interest in this fact as having a possible bearing on the demand for money, and he dismissed it (pages 145–147) by saying that while "credit money" was convenient in facilitating transactions, it has nothing to do with the measure of values, which was his only concern.

No doubt Harvey's conception of money stemmed from a kind of business experience, then only recently outmoded, that still fashioned the thinking of many farmers and some businessmen. His views reflected the folkish feeling that pieces of money are not really "good" unless they have a roughly equivalent value for nonmonetary purposes, or are directly redeemable in money that has such value. "Some years ago," E. Benjamin Andrews reported in 1894, "I found a man who for a decade owned and carried on the chief store in a flourishing New England village, ignorant how to draw a check. If this in the East, how slight must be the play of banking methods in the West and South." [27] Men out of such village backgrounds naturally thought of the solution to monetary problems entirely in terms of primary money, and were

[27] *An Honest Dollar* (Hartford, Conn., 1894), pp. 26–27.

uninterested in the possibilities that lay in devising more flexible instruments of check credit. Perhaps the most severe stricture that can be made against them was that when the nation finally came to the point of trying to devise a mobile credit structure that would make possible a more adequate response to the kind of evil they had protested against, men like Harvey were too firm in their antibank prejudices to applaud the effort, and were to be found instead sniping at it as nothing more than a new source of profits and power for usurers.

At any rate, Harvey's notion that the appreciation of gold was the primary source of the hardships of his time throughout the price-depressed Western world was a rough popular version of a view of the matter taken by many more sophisticated contemporaries in the United States and Europe, among them distinguished economists and statesmen. Such respectable contemporaries were profoundly disturbed by business instability and unemployment and by the widespread and growing discontent of the agricultural populations of several nations. They put a heavy burden of blame for depressed prices on the formation of the international gold standard. As they saw it, each new Western nation that clambered aboard the gold-standard bandwagon after 1873 added its own needs to the general scramble for a very limited supply of gold. The metal appreciated and prices dropped. And certainly, if price stability was the thing most urgently desired, the record of the gold standard in these years and afterwards was not inspiring.[28] Bimetallism, moreover, was a respectable proposition in economic theory, and it is easy to be persuaded that things might have been somewhat better had the nations, say, in the 1870's or even the early 1880's, successfully arrived at an agree-

[28] See, on this count, D. H. Robertson, *Money*, pp. 117–119.

ment to put the Western trading community on a bimetallic basis.

It is impossible for the layman to evaluate the merits of this traditional case against the gold standard. But most economists who are familiar with macroeconomic developments have tended in recent years to minimize the effect of the bullion basis of money in the secular price decline, as compared with certain long-range changes that came with industrialism and improvements in transportation. The development of industry brought many long-range cost-reducing improvements. Massive investments in railroads and shipping, improvements in transportation facilities, the opening of the Suez Canal — such changes led to the rapid development of great tracts of virgin land throughout the world and the rapid shrinkage of the world into a single market. The effects of such changes were felt with special acuteness by the farming populations, which found themselves competing in a crowded international market and victims of a common international agrarian depression. Studies in the history of the real money supply, moreover, indicate that changes in banking during this secular price decline were more and more detaching the real money supply from the rate of growth of the gold supply. The calculations of J. G. Gurley and E. S. Shaw for the United States, which take account of demand deposits and other sources of expansion, show a steady growth in the real per capita money supply for the decades from 1869 to 1899, and an annual rate of growth somewhat higher than in the years before the Civil War.[29] The gold standard may well have

[29] See the two essays by Gurley and Shaw already cited. There is an account of the views of economists on the role of monetary factors in the depression of the 1890's in Rendigs Fels, *American Business Cycles, 1865–1897* (Chapel Hill, N. C., 1959), chapters xi and xii. Charles Hoffman, in "The Depression of the Nineties," *Journal of*

aggravated the price decline but it cannot be assigned full blame.

To accept these findings, however, is not to deny the merit of the demand for inflation in the mid-1890's. There was an excellent case, both economic and moral, for a jolt of controllable inflation that would have stimulated enterprise and readjusted the balance between debtors and creditors. The difficulty was to find a mechanism for such inflation that would have achieved the desired price rise without so dislocating foreign trade and investment and so shaking the confidence of the business community that the anticipated benefits would be undone. Under modern conditions of central banking, the mechanisms are at hand; in the 1890's this was not the case, and so the debate centered around the monetary standard. From the vantage point of a later age there seems to be something genuinely tragic in the clash of the two hypnotic dogmatisms of gold and silver, neither of whose exponents had an adequate comprehension of the problem nor an adequate program for the relief of economic misery.

It is against this background that the true poignancy

Economic History, 16 (June 1956), pp. 137–164, concludes that monetary and fiscal policies were secondary, aggravating forces. Lee Benson summarizes the literature on the transportation revolution and its international consequences in his essay, "The Historical Background of Turner's Frontier Essay," in *Turner and Beard* (Glencoe, Ill., 1960), pp. 42ff; and A. E. Musson does the same for the literature on "The Great Depression in Britain, 1873–1896," *Journal of Economic History*, 19 (June 1959), pp. 199–228. On the limitations of the gold standard in accounting for the secular price decline, see J. T. Phinney, "Gold Production and the Price Level," *Quarterly Journal of Economics*, 47 (August 1933), pp. 647–679; and E. H. Phelps Brown and S. A. Ozga, "Economic Growth and the Price Level," *Economic Journal*, 65 (March 1955), 1–18. Cf. J. M. Keynes, *Treatise on Money* (London, 1930), II, 164–170; and W. T. Layton and Geoffrey Crowther, *An Introduction to the Study of Prices* (London, 1938), chapter viii.

of Harvey's willfully amateur attempt to restate the silver case may be seen. There is, of course, a certain innocent amusement to be had from poking fun at cranks. But when cranks acquire the wide popular following that men like Harvey had, it may be the better part of statesmanship to take their agitations, even if not their ideas, seriously. What was being debated in America and Europe during the 1890's was a major social issue which had its moral side as well as its technical economic dimension. And on the moral side, the defenders of the gold standard often seem as dogmatically sealed within their own premises as the most wild-eyed silver men, and usually less generous in their social sympathies. The right-thinking statesmanship of the era, like its right-thinking economics, was so locked in its own orthodoxy that it was incapable of coming to terms in a constructive way with lasting and pervasive social grievances. The social philosophy of J. Laurence Laughlin and the statecraft of Grover Cleveland cannot, in this respect, command our admiration. They accepted as "natural" a stark, long-range price deflation, identified the interests of creditors with true morality, and looked upon any attempt to remedy the appreciation of debt as unnatural and dishonest, as a simple repudiation of sacred obligations — an attempt, as Laughlin put it in his debate with Harvey, "to transfer from the great mass of the community who have been provident, industrious and successful a portion of their savings and gains into the pockets of those who have been idle, extravagant, or unfortunate." [30] This attitude was as provocative as it was smug, and it was not calculated to engender humane statesmanship. Allan Nevins, un-

[30] *Facts about Money*, p. 233; cf. his comments about "the less fortunate, the less successful, the less wise," and "the greater prosperity of the successful [that] is due to the possession of superior industrial power" in "'Coin's' Food for the Gullible," pp. 574, 576.

stinting though he is in his admiration for Grover Cleveland's defense of the gold standard, remarks that the farmers had legitimate grounds for complaint and that "our history presents few spectacles more ironic than that of their Eastern creditors taunting them with dishonesty while insisting upon being repaid in a dollar far more valuable than had been lent."[31] Laughlin himself put the case in a fairer light when he said: "The highest justice is rendered by the state when it extracts from the debtor at the end of a contract the *same purchasing power* which the creditor gave him at the beginning of the contract, no less, no more," and it is quite understandable why Bryan felt that he was only echoing Laughlin when he said in his speech against repeal of the Sherman Silver Purchase Act: "A dollar approaches honesty as its purchasing power approaches stability."[32]

The international bimetallists seem to have been on sound ground insofar as they saw the future solution to deflation in supranational arrangements that would enable the trading powers to maintain stable exchange rates and yet keep some freedom in domestic price poli-

[31] *Grover Cleveland*, p. 594. Any change in the value of money has the effect of redistributing income among social classes; and changes in the value of money are the consequences, among other things, of the decisions of governments—even if they are only decisions *not* to act. One can readily understand the fury of inflationists, after years of deflationary monetary decisions, at being told that their proposals to raise prices were unwarranted and dishonest efforts to interfere with the course of nature. The gold advocates had taken it upon themselves to define the terms of the controversy in such a way as to make it impossible for them to be wrong.

[32] Laughlin, *The History of Bimetallism*, p. 70; Bryan, *The First Battle*, p. 80. The whole question of the price level as one of both policy and morality is circumspectly discussed in chapter vii of D. H. Robertson's classic exposition, *Money*. See also the grounds for Keynes's conclusion that "it is worse, in an impoverished world, to provoke unemployment than to disappoint the rentier." *Essays in Persuasion* (London, 1931), p. 103.

cies; whereas the dogmatic gold men, who believed that currency was governed by laws so immutable that money was not susceptible to further management, were looking in the wrong direction. Of course, the overwhelming majority of American silver men were not international bimetallists; like Harvey, they were uncompromising advocates of unilateral action. The difference was vital. The international aspect of the problem was the Achilles' heel of the American silver men — and it is no coincidence that when Harvey comes, near the end of *Coin's Financial School,* to the hopeless problem of maintaining bimetallism in one country, he drops his façade of didactic calm and rational argument and breaks into a tirade against England. The idea that the United States, acting alone, could uphold the value of silver and maintain bimetallism, as opposed to adopting silver monometallism, had long been preposterous; the notion that we could coin unlimited amounts of silver at 16 to 1 at a time when the market ratio had dropped to 32 to 1, and still hold to a bimetallic standard, was understandably regarded by its opponents as a form of economic lunacy. For this reason, the "respectable" bimetallists, in the United States as elsewhere, saw the problem of the monetary standard as an international one. On this count they were regarded by the silver nationalists as abject traitors.

The one reality that the silver nationalists would not face was that the course of events since 1871 had so undermined the international position of silver that nothing short of concerted international action could restore it as a standard money. Few of them were candid enough to admit that, because the value of the two metals had so far parted company in the past twenty years, they had in fact become silver monometallists. Today, when we are no longer enthralled by illusions about the perfection or inevitability of the gold standard, it may still be possible to argue speculatively, as a few candid silver men did in 1894, that it would have been healthier to restore prices through silver monometallism than to accept the drastic and disheartening fall in prices that was still going on. But the switch to a silver standard might have been self-defeating simply because of its blow to business confidence. And even if one were to dismiss this intangible, the blows to foreign investment and trade would probably have had repercussions serious enough to delay rather than to hasten recovery. The United States was a debtor nation and an importer of capital; and the effects of a silver standard upon its debt service and the investment market might well have constituted a minor disaster. Abstractly, there was nothing wrong with a silver standard, or for that matter a paper standard, but it does not follow that the shift could have been made without causing, as Senator Cockrell so confidently said, "as much as a ripple in our financial system." [33]

One thing that can be said in the light of historical perspective is that the critical moment for a stand for silver through an international agreement had long since passed. Moreover, the American silver movement itself could be charged with having done its own part to weaken the forces working for such an agreement.

Behind this charge lies a long history of international discussion and negotiation, marked by four international monetary conferences in 1867, 1878, 1881, and 1892. It is true that Britain had steadfastly refused to abandon

[33] Most historians who have discussed the battle of the standards have written largely as ideologists. Liberal historians have treated the subject as though the sufferings of the farmers and the broad social sympathies of the silver men were an adequate substitute for sound remedial proposals—somewhat in the spirit of Vachel Lindsay's

her own gold standard, and her unwillingness to do so had been interpreted, rightly or wrongly, by the other great nations as an insuperable obstacle to satisfactory international action on silver. But, partly because of Britain's growing concern for the stability of silver, a concern arising from her trade with India, which was on a silver standard, British spokesmen would have welcomed action taken by the United States, alone or in concert with other nations, that would have successfully sustained the international use and the price of the white metal. In Britain the gold standard was both a habit and a dogma, but it was not considered to be a proselytizing creed eligible for export.

During the many years when the international bimetallic movement was working for an agreement among the nations on the use of silver, the American silver purchase policy, along with the threat that unlimited coinage might soon follow, had hung like a dark cloud over the international conferences. The more reason the European governments had to expect that American silver purchase policies would give them a dumping ground for their silver and an opportunity to strengthen their gold position, the less likely they were to yield to the arguments of their own bimetallists. American presidents from Hayes to McKinley, sensitive as they were to the political power of silver, had all been interested in efforts to arrive at an international monetary agreement, but their efforts were constantly undermined not

---

fatuous poem, "Bryan, Bryan, Bryan, Bryan." On the other hand, most conservative historians who have written at length about the merits of the monetary controversy itself have quietly assumed that the orthodoxies of J. Laurence Laughlin are still untouched. They would have us enter uncritically into the spirit of Grover Cleveland's assertion that if the United States went off gold, it "could no longer claim a place among nations of the first class."

only by the successes of the silver interests in Congress in 1878 and 1890 but by the indiscreet interventions of silver Congressmen in monetary diplomacy.[34]

Probably the most strategic moment for an international agreement was the conference of 1881, when America's gold position was strong and the European powers were suffering a serious gold crisis. A great wave of bimetallist sentiment swept Europe, from which Britain was by no means immune, and British representatives came to the conference quite interested in seeing the *other* nations, perhaps the United States and the Latin Union, open their mints to unlimited coinage. But current American silver purchases under the Bland-Allison Act checked the silver impetus almost as much as the British refusal to go off gold.

Eleven years later, the British, led by Alfred de Rothschild, a Director of the Bank of England, came to the conference of 1892 still unwilling to change their own standard, but still concerned about the rupee and solicitous about silver.[35] At this meeting they proposed that the Continental nations, together with the United States, should undertake a common program of silver purchases — in support of which the British offered, as their contribution, to raise the amount of silver acceptable as legal tender in England from £2 to £5. This would have been

[34] See Jeannette P. Nichols' account of these interventions in "Silver Diplomacy," *Political Science Quarterly*, 48 (December 1933), 565–588. Henry B. Russell gives a detailed account of the effects of American silver policies on the international meetings in his *International Monetary Conferences* (New York, 1898); see especially pp. 192–199, 249, 260, 323–327, 369, 409–410. Concerning the interventions of the silver men and their effects on the prospects of bimetallism, Russell remarks (pp. 324–325): "No doctrine ever stood in such dire need of being delivered from its most officious friends."

[35] One can only wonder if "Coin" Harvey was aware of the prophetic words of Alfred de Rothschild at this conference, and what

a small price for Britain to pay to relieve the difficulties of her Eastern commerce by inducing the United States to make a firm commitment to silver purchases. British financiers were indeed trying to make use of the resources of the United States — not by forcing this country onto the gold standard, as the American silverites charged, but by getting it pledged to continue the silver purchases of the Sherman Act. The British position was far from disinterested, but it reveals some of the complexities of the economic world that could hardly have been comprehensible to devoted readers of *Coin's Financial School*: "Coin" Harvey, William Jennings Bryan, and Alfred de Rothschild marching arm in arm in a campaign to uphold the American silver purchase policy!

ix

The real world of business and finance was complex, but the mental world of the money agitators was beautifully simple. Among its treasured legends was the idea that the gold standard had been stealthily imposed upon the American people by the British banking powers. The anti-British feeling and the conspiratorial view of monetary history expressed in *Coin's Financial School* were dressed out more elaborately in a propagandistic novel, *A Tale of Two Nations,* which Harvey brought out in September 1894, only three months after the appearance of his masterpiece. This work, possibly the only *roman à*

he would have made of them: "Gentlemen, I need hardly remind you that the stock of silver in the world is estimated at some thousands of millions, and if this conference were to break up without arriving at any definite result there would be a depreciation in the value of that commodity which it would be frightful to contemplate, and out of which a monetary panic would ensue, the far-reaching effects of which it would be impossible to foretell." Russell, *International Monetary Conferences*, p. 385.

clef ever written about the gold standard, deserves attention in its own right. Written more or less at the same time as *Coin's Financial School*, it makes a fuller statement of some of its sentiments, and it must rank in symptomatic significance with Ignatius Donnelly's *Caesar's Column* as a fantasy in fiction that illuminates the populist mind. Harvey himself never lost faith in this novel's importance, for he reprinted it as late as 1931.[36]

A Tale of Two Nations opens in the year 1869, when Baron Rothe (Rothschild), a portly and immensely intelligent banker of an old Jewish house is discussing his plans with another financier, Sir William T. Cline. The Baron has a daring scheme: if silver can be demonetized in the United States and Europe, gold will double its purchasing power, to the immense advantage of gold owners and holders of debts contracted for payment in gold. Here, he says, is a stroke of policy that will do more for England than a thousand years of conquests by arms. The United States, instead of overshadowing England in world trade, would (in some way not clearly specified) find herself impoverished, her industrial power broken. When his guest demurs that a measure of demonetization amounting to financial suicide would never be enacted by the Congress, Baron Rothe confidently replies that almost no one in Congress knows anything about money, and that a bill framed in sufficiently deceptive terms

[36] By all accounts it was the second most successful of his writings in popularity. Priced at fifty cents, it was bought eagerly by his public; and while we may not accept his own estimation of a circulation of 500,000, the second edition alone appears to have run to at least one fifth of that figure, and there were other editions. The book had the advantage of being advertised in later editions of *Coin's Financial School* as "THE MOST EXCITING AND INTERESTING NOVEL ON AMERICAN POLITICS EVER PUBLISHED." In fact, Harvey appended to such editions the first two chapters of *A Tale of Two Nations* to titillate his readers.

would go through; its real effects would not be discovered for years. Ruthlessly the Baron outlines his plans: the power of money, skillfully used, would "establish two classes, the rich and the poor. The first to enjoy this world, and the other to live by waiting on the first. We must crush their manhood by making them poor — they then will make good servants and gentle citizens."

The first instrument of this cold-blooded plot is an American Senator, John Arnold (John Sherman and Benedict Arnold?), who now visits Baron Rothe in London. Arnold puts up the appearance of noble American statesmanship, but his true character is read by Baron Rothe and by the baron's beautiful daughter Edith. This dark lady has powers of character diagnosis that are practically occult; she quickly finds that Arnold is a consummate worshipper of the power of money. Baron Rothe has no difficulty in bribing Arnold to use his influence to work for the demonetization of silver. Three years later the conspiracy brings to Washington the young nephew of the baron, one Victor Rogasner, a darkly handsome cosmopolitan of sybaritic tendencies, whose mission is to forward the final passage of the demonetization measure. Rogasner is aided by a secretary, by two former Scotland Yard men, whose business it is to work on Congressmen, and by a passionate and beautiful Russian Jewess who will do anything necessary to advance the projects or achieve the happiness of the man she loves. Rogasner is full of guile and the spirit of vengeance. "In the highest sense I am a military commander," he muses:

> I am here to destroy the United States—Cornwallis could not have done more. For the wrongs and insults, for the glory of my own country, I will bury the knife deep into the heart of this nation . . . I will crush their manhood. I will destroy the last vestige of national prosperity among them, and humble that

accursed pride with which they refer to their revolutionary ancestors, to the very dust. I will set them fighting among each other, and see them cut each other's throats, and carry devastation into each other's homes, while I look on without loss.

In the corrupt atmosphere of the Grant administration, which Harvey fills in with a few hasty strokes, it becomes quite plausible that still another, unknown, scandal, based on the quest for favorable monetary legislation by the gold interests, could actually have taken place. Rogasner has his moments of doubt and suspense, but before long his strategy carries the day — silver is demonetized, the Crime of '73 is a fact. "The greatest crime ever committed in the world — one that was to cause more suffering than all other crimes committed in a century, had been quietly accomplished." The American Congressmen do not yet know what they have done, and it takes them three years to discover it. Later Rogasner is instrumental in securing the demonetization of silver in Germany (anachronistically) and France. He then returns to the United States to wage a propaganda battle in favor of the gold standard, because silver advocates are now up in arms. But it proves easy to suborn professors of economics and the greater part of the press. The people are "helpless victims in the power of a soulless gold oligarchy."

The story jumps to 1894, and new characters are introduced. The corrupt Senator Arnold has a ward, Grace Vivian; and Rogasner, now a man of great affluence, in his middle years but still handsome, takes a fancy to her. Grace prefers the attentions of John Melwyn, a noble, handsome, well-proportioned, and eloquent young silverite Congressman from Lincoln, Nebraska, who resembles William Jennings Bryan. The contest, nonetheless, seems unequal: Rogasner is rich and Melwyn is poor, and, what is more, Rogasner is wily. American innocence is once more at a disadvantage in confronting European duplicity. "The honest heart and frank directness of the younger man; his simple rearing, uneventful, in a sense, furnished few weapons with which to meet the wily diplomacy and cunning, the broad knowledge and teachings of a life of intrigue, possessed by the polished nephew of Baron Rothe." Worst of all, Senator Arnold cannot bear Melwyn's free silver views. In this contest between the Englishman and the American for a girl "fair and beautiful enough to typify Columbia," the unscrupulous Senator secretly intercepts Melwyn's letters, in order to give Grace the impression that Melwyn has lost interest in her.

The story moves towards its climax against a background of the stirring events of 1894 — the suffering brought by the panic, the fear awakened by the march of Coxey's army on Washington, the bitterness aroused by the Pullman strike. Melwyn's brother turns up as a member of Coxey's army, his father too is ruined, and Melwyn himself is plagued by a mortgage he cannot pay, unaware that the long arm of Rogasner is stiffening the demands of his creditors. Rogasner, hardhearted as ever in the midst of all the distress of the depression years, waits for the day when seventy per cent of the people are in distress — at which point, he believes, the political situation will explode, and the present government of the United States will either be supplanted by a monarchy or completely consumed in a revolution. Meanwhile, as the people worry about a variety of unimportant issues, and are thus distracted from the fundamental money question, "we are shooting from ambush, and are perfectly safe . . . I shall sink this accursed nation; tear it into threads, and leave it bleeding and disrupted, if for no other purpose than to demonstrate the power of our money."

In an interesting passage, Rogasner pursues a line of thought that sheds light on Harvey's conception of the gold conspirators. For Rogasner proves to be a man who understands full well, with the immemorial wisdom and historic consciousness of the Jew ("it takes one of our race [Jesus] to detect this error in our civilization [usury]"), that lending and hoarding since the times of the Medes and Persians has been the root cause of the breakdown of civilizations. He is even clever enough to outline — in private — a Harveyesque scheme for a "perfect civilization" based on the abolition of debt and usury and the heavy taxation of wealth. Still, knowing the path to perfection as he does, he chooses evil. He is an angel of darkness, a Manichean nightmare.[37]

[37] Like the other political characters in the book, Rogasner was probably intended to represent an actual person. It was part of the legend of many true believers in the silver cause that a London banker, Ernest Seyd, had come to the United States with $500,000 which he used to bribe Congressmen to pass the Coinage Act of 1873. The silver men even purported to have an affadavit from a Denver businessman to show that Seyd had later privately confessed to having played such a role. This version of the passage of the Crime of '73 was quite common in silver tracts, and Harvey could hardly have missed it. (The most ample statement I have seen is in Gordon Clark's *Handbook of Money*, n.p., published by the Silver Knight Publishing Company, 1896, pp. 189–206.)

Seyd was in fact a London banker, born in Germany, who had lived in the United States for many years, and had been in business in San Francisco. There is no reliable evidence that he was in the United States in 1872, but he was consulted by Representative Samuel C. Hooper about the Coinage Act of 1873, and wrote him a long, technical letter about it, February 17, 1872, in which he advised, among other things, the *reintroduction* of the long defunct silver dollar at what he regarded a more practicable weight, and a firm commitment to bimetallism. See *Documentary History of the Coinage Act of February 12, 1873* (Washington, U.S. Printing Office, n.d. [1894?]), pp. 95–106; cf. Seyd's *Suggestions in Reference to the*

But his personal defeat awaits him. After an assiduous courtship he at last hungrily proposes to Grace ("The man's eyes blazed with the fire of his race in the old days, the fire that came when David gazed upon Bathsheba, or when the eyes of Jacob first rested on Rachel at the well"). She politely refuses, saying that she would just like to be "good friends." Growing desperate, he now reveals to her for the first time his true identity: he is not an American investment counselor at all, as his conspiratorial activities have required him to pretend; he tells her of his aristocratic family and his wealth and prospects, hoping to appeal to the fortune-hunter or title-hunter that is supposed to lurk in almost every American girl. "I come from one of the oldest and proudest and wealthiest of European families. In fact the oldest and wealthiest in the world. Our millions aid in controlling the affairs of nations . . . In time I will be a baron."

Metallic Coinage of the United States of America (London, 1871), and his letter to the Monetary Commission of 1876, U.S. Congress, 44th Congress, 2nd sess., Senate Report 703, *Documents Accompanying the Report of the U.S. Monetary Commission*, II, 106–135.

Seyd, who died in 1881, was a Fellow of the Royal Statistical Society and one of the better-known British bimetallists. Most of the silver men who discussed the subject were aware of Seyd's lifelong advocacy of bimetallism, but in their view this by no means ruled out the possibility that his fealty to the British gold power was stronger than his personal convictions. Had they not seen men like Secretary Carlisle converted from solid bimetallists into defenders of the gold standard? Like Rogasner, Seyd could know good and do evil. As Gordon Clark wrote of Seyd: "That very able acquaintance of the Rothschilds—a gentleman of the same Hebrew blood—was no disburser of bribes, in ordinary circumstances, and was a *sincere bimetallist*. But he was also 'the financial adviser of the Bank of England,'" and in this capacity, "was forced to postpone his theories when that huge octopus came to see its fat prey in the United States" (pp. 195–196).

The Seyd story became the object of some discussion on the floor of Congress in 1890 and again in 1893. For the latter, see *Congressional Record*, 53rd Congress, 1st sess., pp. 474–476, 584–589, 1059.

Rogasner has overplayed his hand; Grace is offended at this attempt to buy her. "You sneer at America and talk of a better civilization of which you say I may be made an ornament. I am proud of being an American woman and I am content with this civilization of which you speak so lightly. It may be barbarous, but I am content." Now Rogasner plays his ace. He goes to Senator Arnold, asking for his intercession. But the Senator, whose one uncorrupted emotion is his affection for his ward, feels that he cannot try to determine her choice of a husband. At home again, Rogasner broods over the possibility of a last resort — blackmailing the Senator with his knowledge of the Senator's corruption. Rogasner's brother, a minor figure in the demonetization conspiracy, chides him for his obsession with Grace: "Are there not women of our own race and faith beautiful enough and with all grace of mind and body to fit them for any man?" But Rogasner is unmoved: "Did not our ancestors, even on Arabian plains, take whatever women of whatever race most pleased their fancy?" Rogasner proceeds to blackmail Senator Arnold, and the threat of exposure reduces the Senator to prostration. Rogasner gloats like the fiend he is — he "was not exactly smiling — he was leering, and he was as happy as Nero was in the death agonies of his mother. The Hebrew was 'harrowing' again." But Grace has overheard his words, and she breaks in on the two men, reproaching her guardian, and upbraiding Rogasner: "You are very shrewd. You are very wise in your way, the commercial way, inbred through generations. The politic, scheming, devious way inbred through generations also. You are as repulsive to me as anything that could exist." As Rogasner arises and approaches her — with who knows what intent — none other than John Melwyn, "the typical American man," breaks in and throws him to the floor.

There is little more to be told. John Melwyn and Grace marry, and Rogasner goes back home to the selfless Jeanne Soutleffsky, "the fair Jewess who had been his agent in so many instances," and who was there to welcome him "like Rebecca solicitous over Ivanhoe." She has patiently endured his pursuit of Grace Vivian, and now "her face was a poem, a great epic poem of the grand old Jewish race." Rogasner needs her: he breaks down and becomes a helpless invalid, and benefits for the rest of his life from her devotion. The book ends on what Harvey's silverite readers must have felt was a chilling note: "On the 29th day of September, 1894, there sailed on the steamer Paris from Liverpool a representative of a foreign syndicate to take Rogasner's place."

The mild note of anti-Semitism in Harvey's book will not surprise those who are familiar with the traditional linkage of money crazes and anti-Jewish feeling. In the American silver movement this prejudice was a facet of the far more deeply felt anti-British sentiment; it did not go beyond a kind of rhetorical vulgarity, since no programmatic steps were urged against Jews as such. Like such a Populist contemporary as Ignatius Donnelly, Harvey had mixed feelings and showed a certain shame about his prejudice which caused him to interlard his anti-Semitic remarks with awkward philo-Semitic amends. In *Coin's Financial School Up to Date*[38] Harvey disavowed prejudice against the Jews —

> the brightest race of people that inhabit the earth, and they treat each other with the greatest fairness as a rule . . . You should not be prejudiced against any race as a race . . . Among the Jews, many became money changers; it seems to be natural

[38] (Chicago, 1895), p. 68. On the similar ambivalence of Ignatius Donnelly, see Martin Ridge, *Ignatius Donnelly* (Chicago, 1962), pp. 263–264, 266n, 305, 321–323, 336–337, 395–396. C. Vann Woodward

with them, probably on account of their excessive shrewdness. They see that it has advantages not possessed by any other business.

Many Jews, it must be said, might have found Harvey's embraces harder to endure than his slurs.

In the end, Harvey could not untangle himself from the Shylock image, which pervades money crankery from the Greenbackers to Father Coughlin and Ezra Pound, and his later writings are dotted with repetitive citations of prohibitions against usury on the part of Christian thinkers. In his *Common Sense, or The Clot on the Brain of the Body Politic*,[39] he borrowed a quotation used in Redpath's *History of the World* which stated that the Jew does not work as most men do, contributes nothing to human industry, but "obtains control of the money market, using the same for the exclusive advantage of himself and his people." In spite of the repeated injunctions of the Christian Churches against usury down through the ages, Harvey said, the rules of the Christian churches "ever had a persistent enemy following them and seeking to loan money — taking pledges, binding borrowers to secrecy and adding to their stock of money till by the 17th century their holdings were enough to choke civilization to a favorable concession." Here he quoted the central passage on usury from Deuteronomy 23: 19, 20, in which usury within the tribe is forbidden, but in which what he called the "fatal exception" was made: "Unto a stranger thou mayest lend upon usury."[40] This, he declared, "made money-lenders of the Jews. Re-

---

has pointed out that the Populists had no monopoly on anti-Semitism in the 1890's. See his remarks in *The Burden of Southern History* (Baton Rouge, La., 1960), pp. 154–155.

[39] (Monte Ne, Ark., 1920), p. 18.

[40] On the historic interpretation of the Deuteronomic prohibition, see Benjamin F. Nelson, *The Idea of Usury* (Princeton, 1949).

garding the Gentiles as 'strangers,' their enemies, they have sought to punish them, to ruin them, with the weapon usury." But there is still hope for the Jews if they will relent and reform:

A stricken world cries out to them to make public renunciation of usury and to make *restitution* by crowding into the front ranks of reformers against the sin! The Jews come of a noble race, possessing a high order of intelligence, acumen and persistency in a cause; and by recognizing that it is inconsistent with the 'brotherhood of man' to wield the Sword of 'Usury' against the Gentiles, they will assimilate into the activities of productive civilization, be worthy descendants of their pastoral forefathers, and will become vocationally adapted to the cultivation and rebuilding of their ancient land.

X

During his celebrity as a silver tractarian Harvey was also briefly active in politics. In 1894, he was busy with the affairs of the Populist party of Illinois, which, unlike most other state Populist parties, had a strong labor-socialist wing interested in writing a collectivist plank into the party's program. Harvey's sympathies lay with the more conservative agrarian wing of the party, which repudiated collectivism and put its hopes in monetary reform. When the two factions of the Illinois party finally fell out, he joined with the Prohibitionist leader, Howard S. Taylor, in curbing the radicals. In 1895 he published *Coin's Financial School Up to Date*, in which Coin returns to expound Harvey's financial ideas in a work marked by a long discussion of greed and ignorance as forces in history, and by attacks on British landholders in the United States. During the same year, Harvey conducted a debate on the silver issue with J. Laurence Laughlin and a series of nine debates with ex-Congressman Roswell H. Horr. He also tried to organize a kind of political fraternal order, open to members of all existing parties, which he hoped to purify. The organization was to be called The Patriots of America, and its lodges were to have their own ritual, somewhat in the fashion of national fraternal orders; there was to be a kind of women's auxiliary, the Daughters of the Republic. Harvey's book, *The Patriots of America,* was devoted in large part to a proposed constitution for this order, and pending an election, he offered himself as its First National Patriot. *The Patriots of America* suffered an excess of incoherence that was to envelop Harvey's later writings, and from a striking note of exaggeration, grandiosity, and suspicion. Good and evil were struggling for the control of the world, he held, and things had become so bad that "we must make the last stand of freemen for the civilization of the world." Murders, suicides, crime, insanity, and British and railroad landholdings were all strung together as evidences of the pathological state society had reached: "The United States has been honeycombed by foreign influences and our property is rapidly passing into their hands." [41]

Some features of Harvey's proposed Patriots of America, especially its semisecrecy, worried Bryan and his supporters, who saw in it a possible source of factionalism. Harvey explained that the organization would "give us the finances for a national campaign" against the money power, and that its secrecy and its required pledge that members must vote in conformity with majority decisions were intended to foil "cunning and unscrupulous" enemies from working within the ranks. "I love you," wrote Harvey to Bryan, "and shall always have your good in view because I believe you to be one of the first patriots in the country." [42]

[41] *The Patriots of America* (Chicago, 1895), pp. 12, 28, 39–40.
[42] Nichols, "Bryan's Benefactor," pp. 321–322.

During 1896, Harvey worked fervently for Bryan, giving lectures and speeches and distributing silver badges. Harvey (who had originally preferred "Silver Dick" Bland of Missouri) was then a member of the executive committee of the National Silver party, which bought a million copies of Archbishop Walsh's *Bimetallism and Monometallism*, half in English and half in a German translation, as well as 125,000 copies of *Coin's Financial School*.[43] After the campaign, Harvey spent some months lecturing to raise money for the Democrats. His cordial relations with Bryan continued, and as late as 1913 Bryan was still trying to secure for him a post in the department of Agriculture under Woodrow Wilson.[44]

The year 1896 was the zenith of the silver cause. In the following year the tide of depression turned. New gold deposits and new methods of extraction hastened a rise in prices that the silver men had thought could come only from the white metal. It soon became apparent that silver was a lost cause, that the ground had been cut from under men who whole intellectual and political lives had hung upon monetary agitation. Chicago, the scene of his one great success, began to pall for Harvey. In 1899, he published the last book to appear under the aegis of the Coin Publishing Company, *Coin on Money, Trusts and Imperialism*.

Coin, now supposedly a youth of sixteen, returns in this volume for a last effort to stem the tide of reaction. He presents human history as an arena of struggle between two types of people — the humane type, that delights in the upbuilding of mankind without neglecting

[43] Bryan, *The First Battle*, p. 292.

[44] Much to the irritation of Secretary of Agriculture David F. Houston, who had always regarded Harvey and his famous book as "huge jokes." D. F. Houston, *Eight Years with Wilson's Cabinet* (New York, 1926), I, 43.

self, and the selfish type, that seeks only self-promotion and self-aggrandizement. The first of these forces is now animating the movement for democracy and reform, the second expresses itself in the cry for monarchy and imperialism. Some considerable portion of the book is, of course, given over to Coin's views on money and banking, but it suffers from its lack of concentration on a single theme. It moves on to attack British investors in America and British holders of American land, and then to denounce the British government for permitting money-lenders to shape the laws. Coin then passes on to the trust question, at the time a matter of growing public concern, but Harvey was much less at home with this issue than with money: his main suggestion was that all industrial trusts are nourished by the financial trust, and if the financial trust can be destroyed, the others will disappear with it.

Moving on to imperialism, the great issue of the moment, Coin saw the drive toward imperialism in rather vague moral terms: an evil genius entrenched in the nation's monetary and industrial system naturally sought to extend itself. "A selfish force having despoiled its own people, seeks other people whom it may despoil. Having preyed upon its own people, with an enlarged appetite, it looks about for other peoples to prey upon — which is called *conquest*." What Coin now began to designate in plain Manichean terms as "the Evil influence" was invoked to explain the development of the Spanish war into an imperial enterprise. As a war in behalf of a victimized Cuban people against a dissolute Spanish monarchy, Coin, in common with so many Americans, saw the Spanish war as being justified. But privileged classes had seized upon it to take the first step toward installing monarchy in the United States by moving into the Philippines and by keeping the United States in Cuba. Many people, Harvey thought, like expansion because they think it will improve business. In fact, there is ample room within the United States for indefinite expansion, and prosperity can be stimulated by home improvements. He recommended a canal to connect Lake Michigan with Lake Erie and the development of a system of good roads and irrigation ditches.

The emotional climax of the volume occurs at a point at which Coin links American occupation of the Philippines with the British war against the Boers and indicts President McKinley for showing sympathy for England and following her example. Coin cries:

> I arraign the President *for treason* in waging a war without that war having first been declared by Congress, as required by the Constitution! I arraign him for treason for a *secret alliance* with England against Republics struggling for liberty! I arraign the majority in Congress as the willing puppets of the Evil influence that prompts the President!

This brings the imaginary audience to its feet, cheering and applauding.

One of Harvey's most urgent worries was that expansionism would bring an enlarged standing army of as many as 100,000 men. He believed, as the Founding Fathers had believed, in a citizen soldiery, in state troops. A standing army under national control might well become the instrument of "monarchy," and certainly it would create a mercenary soldiery, dangerous to domestic government and likely to heighten the desire for conquest. Unlike mercenaries, citizen soldiers would refuse to engage in wars of conquest. "Any war that our citizen soldiers will not fight is an unjust war!" The demand for a standing army was only incidental to the struggle about to open. "Monarchy is ready to spring at the throat of the Republic!" The privileged few, in their quest for subjugation of the people, have only begun with their demand for a standing army. "If they carry the presidential election in 1900, in four years more, they will disclose openly their desire for a Monarchy! . . . The forces of Evil we are combating are organized, and determined of purpose to enslave America!" Harvey left no doubt about what their instrument was: having failed to take over the Democratic party, they had entrenched themselves among the Republicans. Mark Hanna, the symbol of their intentions, had "a bed in the White House . . . patterned after the style of the bed the Queen of England sleeps in."[45] The crying need of the hour was to keep the Democratic party pure, to tighten its organization, and to rally for victory.

xi

Even before Bryan's second defeat in 1900 it must have become apparent to Harvey that no victory was to be expected. In March the confident Republicans easily put through the Gold Standard Act, which, while it was largely a formal declaration of a fact already established, seemed to drive the last nail in the coffin of the silver issue. Two months later, Harvey was preparing to retreat from Chicago. In May 1900 he appeared in the Ozark Mountain town of Rogers, Arkansas, which he had visited in 1894 and 1896 during his campaigns for silver, and rather abruptly bought a tract of 325 acres in a pleasant and well-watered site then called Silver Springs. In the fall he returned with his family, and announced a plan to open an Ozark summer resort outside Rogers. Soon he had renamed his property Monte Ne

[45] *Coin on Money, Trusts, and Imperialism* (Chicago, 1899), pp. 5–6, 9, 31–41, 78, 107, 135, 142–143, 157, 160–161, 171.

(which he imagined meant "mountain of waters" in Spanish) and had formed the Monte Ne investment company in concert with two secretaries he had brought from his Chicago enterprises. The following spring, Hotel Monte Ne was opened, and before long it rang with the tunes of oldtime fiddlers whom Harvey had imported in his hope that a revival of old-fashioned rural entertainment would enliven the resort. Visitors arriving at the resort were ferried across the lake by Venetian gondoliers.

Other enterprises followed — a four mile railroad spur to Lowell was built in 1902 to bring visitors to this isolated resort area. William Jennings Bryan came as a speaker at its opening. Excursions were planned with the help of the Frisco railroad, bringing vacationers from Joplin, Fort Smith, and Springfield. With some local entrepreneurs, Harvey organized the Bank of Monte Ne, capitalized at $25,000, and built a white, boxlike structure to house it. He also began to build a huge, rambling hotel consisting of a number of ranges of log cottages, and organized a mercantile company to bring supplies into Monte Ne.

For a few years it must have seemed that Harvey might begin a wholly new career in the resort business with capital saved from the silver days. But ill luck, personal and financial, seemed to dog him. His family had hardly been long in Monte Ne before the homestead acquired with the Silver Springs tract burned down, destroying Harvey's library, the family piano, silverware, and other household effects brought from Chicago. In 1903, his twenty-three year old son Halliday, who was studying for the law, was killed in a railroad accident. A campaign Harvey planned to make for Congress in 1904 was quickly abandoned in the face of obstinate local rebuffs. In time the Frisco railroad grew tired of running unprofitable excursion trains, and it became increasingly difficult to attract visitors to the splendid isolation of Monte Ne. Harvey's own little railroad failed, and his bank, with all depositors paid in full, closed in 1914. Some part of the projected great hotel was finished, and it was operated with modest success for a period of years, but, in the words of a local chronicler,[46]

> after the foundation for the big hotel was well under way, Mr. Harvey ran into a lot of trouble with union labor organizers, and he abandoned the project and left the masonry for future generations to ponder over its origin and intent. That labor row rather soured Mr. Harvey in his outlook on life and affected all his later years at Monte Ne . . . From this time until his death, Mr. Harvey's life was filled with financial difficulties, legal entanglements over the control of his properties, and the numerous changes in his ambitions.

The handicap arising from Monte Ne's isolation stimulated the last successful effort in Harvey's life, his organization of the Ozark Trails Association to mark and promote 1,500 miles of automobile highways, connecting four towns and five million people in the states of Arkansas, Missouri, Kansas, and Oklahoma. He had seen the railroad fail as a source of transportation for his locality, and it had become evident to any man of vision by 1910, when he first conceived of the Ozark Trails Association, that the automobile was America's coming mode of travel. "My personal interest in the Ozark Trails," Harvey wrote, "is that they all lead to Monte Ne, where we have a delightful resort." For many years after 1913,

[46] The *Rogers Daily News*, July 1, 1950, a local commemorative issue, which contains news stories, pictures, and reminiscences, is my main source for this last phase of Harvey's life. Some gleanings are also to be found in his periodical, *The Palladium*, published at intervals in 1920 and 1925, and in Joseph E. Reeve, *Monetary Reform Movements* (Washington, D.C., 1943).

when he organized the Ozark Trails Association at a meeting held in Monte Ne, Harvey gave his energies to the good-roads movement without expectation of immediate profit. In the hope of bringing what he characteristically called "a vast network of modern auto routes into Arkansas," he spent a great deal of time mapping out and actually marking automobile roads, as well as in strenuous efforts to get the backing of businessmen in adjacent cities. For fifteen years Harvey gave unstintingly of his time, receiving in return only the expenses he incurred while actually engaged in travel, road marking, and promotional activities. What was left of his hotel business apparently suffered from the diversion of his energies, but this identification with a thriving cause once again seems to have mobilized the promotional enthusiasm that had always been so strong in him. "When actively in the harness," wrote one of his co-workers in the good-roads movement, "he seemed to be immune to physical discomfort or fatigue. He had an indomitable will, a crusading spirit, and a great reserve of physical power. In the midst of an important campaign, his eyes would burn with the intense fervor of a mystic." [47] This work was largely done by 1920, and Harvey was again free to devote his energy to his agitations.

Harvey's crusading spirit had not been detached from social issues. He never gave up the hope that the world might be induced to listen, that the success of *Coin's Financial School* could somehow be repeated. In 1915 he began publishing again, with a book entitled *The Remedy*, whose title suggests the hopes he still cherished. *The Remedy* expounded his notion that the forces of Good

[47] Quoted by Clara B. Kennan, "The Ozark Trails and Arkansas's Pathfinder, Coin Harvey," *Arkansas Historical Quarterly*, 7 (Winter 1948), 312–313.

could be strengthened in their battle with Evil by a system of character building in the schools. It incorporated a manual for school instruction in character. In 1920, in his *Common Sense, or The Clot on the Brain of the Body Politic,* he resumed his polemics against selfishness and usury, reviewed the history of money and banking in the United States, and waged a polemic against banking profits under the Federal Reserve system. The Federal Reserve system, he argued, "overshadows the Bank of England, and gives to the money-lenders greater advantage than the old United States bank did, that General Jackson killed. The money-lenders' organization of the banking system may now be regarded as perfected." In his indiscriminate opposition to banks, Harvey was opposing the creation of credit instruments intended to alleviate the very ills that had originally provoked him into becoming a crusader. In this work the paranoid and apocalyptic note sounds stronger than before. Harvey becomes increasingly concerned not merely with Christian prohibitions against usury but with the terrible and sometimes mysterious fate that overcame early opponents of usurious exploitation. Repeatedly he compares the situation of the United States with that of Rome during the persecutions of the Christians:

> The usurers, the money-power in New York City, Chicago, and the large money-lending cities put out the propaganda based on falsehood and misrepresentation as to what the reformers are teaching—as they did in Rome—till the public mind is poisoned and prejudiced and a fair trial is impossible. By suppressing free speech, free press, peaceable assembly, imprisoning and exiling, *the truth is not heard!*

He had become more and more obsessed by the violence and torture inflicted by the Roman empire, and warned that it was likely to be repeated. ("The blood of the martyred Christians appeals to the people of the world in this second Crisis!") He saw the persecution of the early Christians as a political event, a response primarily to their protest against usury, and he cited Tacitus to warn what fate such protest could expect: "Some were nailed on crosses, others sewn up in the skins of wild beasts and exposed to the fury of dogs; others, again smeared over with combustible materials, were used as torches to illuminate the darkness of the night."[48] It is a melancholy thought that this old man, spending his last years in the quiet of an Ozark village, should have had to be tormented by such nightmares.

In 1924, aroused by the postwar depression and a new collapse in American agriculture, Harvey brought out, through his Mundus Publishing Company, a little book called *Paul's School of Statesmanship,* in which another fantastic boy, modeled somewhat after Coin, appears in Monte Ne as Coin had appeared in Chicago, and opens another school. This book, which Harvey said "discloses the most important discovery, relating to civilization and the human race, that has been made in all the history of the world," did not have the reception that its importance warranted. In good part, Paul's was a school of character. He promised a government without taxation or bond issues in a new society, based on gold, of all things, but whose real source of success was the liberal issue of paper currency. The proper understanding of the function of money, Harvey proposed once again, was the key to civilization, but in spite of his promises of a new civilization based upon the solution of the money question, the book showed that Harvey was more than ever

[48] The theme of martyrdom, and his own identification with Christ, is apparent as early as 1895 in "'Coin's Financial School' and its Censors," already cited.

persuaded that a total collapse of civilization would result from the rejection of his views. It was followed six years later by a work entitled, with the simple unaffected confidence of a major prophet, *The Book,* in which Harvey restated many of his old ideas, reused many of his old quotations, rehearsed the historic Christian opposition to usury, warned against dictatorship, reprinted part of *A Tale of Two Nations,* retold the story of the Crime of '73, and called for a new political party.

By now Harvey's faith in the possibility of social reform had grown dimmer. To quote again the local chronicler of his fortunes: "As he grew older and more bitter in his condemnation of existing laws and conditions, he dropped his wealthy friends of these early [business] experiments at Monte Ne and sought the dimes and quarters of the poorer people." In his sixties, Harvey was returning to the agitational frame of mind in which he had come to Chicago, but without the optimism of his earlier days. A civilization incapable of solving the money question was almost certainly headed for disaster. A new vision, announced as early as 1920, began to form in his brain and grew in obsessive strength with the years: he would build in Monte Ne, at the site of his resort, a great Pyramid, in which he would leave copies of his own books, and a variety of artifacts representative of the twentieth-century civilization that he was sure would go to ruin. Thus a future civilization "rising from the ashes" would be able to stumble upon the relics of the past, preserved by "Coin" Harvey. As the years went by his obsession with the Pyramid grew. It would be built of Portland cement, and would be designed to last a million years or longer. It would be forty feet square at the base and rise to 130 feet in height, and at the top, where it would presumably protrude above the dust of the ages, there would be a plaque, reading: "When this can be read go below and find the cause of the death of a former Civilization." Below, the men of the future would find copies of *Paul's School of Statesmanship, The Book*, and the Bible, treated so as to survive time, along with various volumes on the technical and scientific attainments of twentieth-century civilization, and — a thoughtful precaution — a key to the English language so that the works left there would be the more readily decipherable if found by men of a strange tongue.

To raise money to build such a Pyramid, Harvey solicited contributions from the readers of his books. It would be a boon to a later millennium, he pointed out, and "there will be nothing about it that partakes of self or vanity and no one's name will appear on the outside of it." Construction of the Pyramid was actually begun to Harvey's specifications. To make a secure footing for it, he excavated the hills near his home and built what he liked to call the "foyer" of the Pyramid — "an asymmetrical mass of concrete and stone in the form of seats," as a local reporter described it, "but without any semblance of regular order." In surviving pictures it appears like the village of some strange breed of midget Pueblos with disordered minds. At length, with its total estimated cost set at $100,000, this project too was abandoned, like Harvey's hotel and his bank and his railroad — but here, at last, he had an unexpected stroke of luck. The "foyer" itself became a kind of curiosity, a substitute for antique ruins, and thousands of visitors were drawn to them, paying admission fees to gaze upon the fragments of Harvey's unrealized dream. They were treated to lectures on financial reform and given the opportunity to buy Harvey's books, old and new, all conveniently displayed.

By the mid-1920's Harvey had given up all business activities and had yielded completely to his messianic dreams. He attempted through his later writings to organize a new national political party, first called the Liberty party and later the Prosperity party. Perhaps he sought advice from "General" Jacob Coxey, who visited him on occasions to discuss old times and bemoan the condition of the world. The Great Depression of the 1930's gave him a last moment of public notice. In 1932 he ran for president and received 800 votes without campaigning. Three years later he reappeared to denounce Roosevelt's policy of silver purchases, which he regarded as absurdly cautious, a "travesty" on silver. In February 1936, forty years after the battle of the standards, Harvey died at the age of 84. To the end he never lost the pride and sense of his importance that had made it possible for him, against all the probabilities, to claim the attention of the world. A photograph taken in his later years shows a slender, hawk-nosed man still erect and alert, his face adorned by a dignified white mustache, his brow slightly furrowed, his mien a little apprehensive and harassed, looking very much the part of the small-town businessman or banker. Though he was only of medium size, an acquaintance said, "he stood and walked so straight he gave the impression of being taller than his real height." It was as though by a sheer effort of will he could add a cubit to his stature.

April 1963 Richard Hofstadter

A NOTE ON THE TEXT

The hundreds of thousands of copies of *Coin's Financial School* appearing over a span of years after 1894 were all printed by William Harvey's private Coin Publishing Company in Chicago. Printing numbers and dates were not recorded in the volumes, yet minor changes continually appeared and revisions were introduced and discarded.

The copy chosen for reissue here is the earliest complete copy in Harvard University, received March 31, 1895. This printing contains all of the major sections that were a permanent part of the book: omitted from the reissue are the two opening chapters of *A Tale of Two Nations* which Harvey inserted after the final pages of *Coin's Financial School* with other advertisements. The page numbers of the original have been reset into sequence, and the Introduction refers to the new edition. The original index has been reproduced with the new pagination. The clarity of type of the early printing has made it otherwise particularly suitable for photographic reproduction.

A Book that will create a profound impression throughout the United States. **25 Cents.**

—*Chicago Times.*

It mercilessly scourges the money changers in the Temple of the Republic.

—*New York Recorder.*

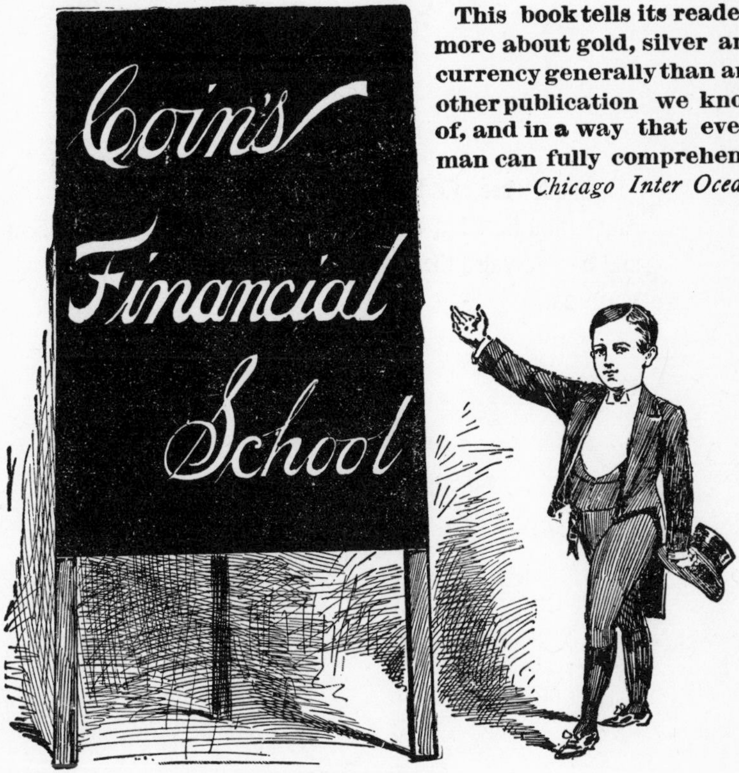

This book tells its readers more about gold, silver and currency generally than any other publication we know of, and in a way that every man can fully comprehend.

—*Chicago Inter Ocean.*

PUBLISHERS:

COIN PUBLISHING COMPANY,

115 MONROE STREET,

CHICAGO.

COIN'S FINANCIAL SERIES, Issued Quarterly. Price, $1.00 per Year. Vol. 1. No. 3, June, 1894

Entered at the Postoffice, Chicago, as second-class mail matter.

I thank thee, O Father, Lord of Heaven and Earth, because thou hast hid these things from the wise and prudent, and hast revealed them unto babes.—MATTHEW, Chapter xi., Verse 25.

HOARDING GOLD.

All Money

IS A MEDIUM OF EXCHANGE,

BUT **Primary Money only**

IS THE MEASURE OF VALUES.

ALL THE GOLD IN THE WORLD IN THE CHICAGO WHEAT PIT.

To Those - - - -

Trying to locate the seat of the disease that threatens the life of the nation, this book is

- - - DEDICATED.

PREFACE.

COLUMBUS DISCOVERING AMERICA. 1492.

At the Christian era the metallic money of the Roman empire amounted to $1,800,000,000. By the end of the fifteenth century it had shrunk to $200,000,000. (Dr. Adam Smith informs us that in 1455 the price of wheat in England was two pence per bushel.) Population dwindled, and commerce, arts, wealth and freedom all disappeared. The people were reduced by poverty and misery to the most degraded conditions of serfdom and slavery. The disintegration of society was almost complete. History records no such disastrous transition as that from the Roman empire to the dark ages. The discovery of the New World by Columbus, restored the volume of precious metals, brought with it rising prices, enabled society to reunite its shattered links, shake off the shackles of feudalism, and to relight and uplift the almost extinguished torch of civilization.—*Report U.* S. *Monetary Commission of 1878.*

STATUE OF COLUMBUS AT CHICAGO. 1893.

The New World in 1893 celebrated the discovery of America by Columbus, during a period of depression brought about by the destruction by law of one-half the precious metals as primary money. So blighting and destructive is the effect, the people are being reduced to poverty and misery; the conditions of life are so hard that individual selfishness is the only thing consistent with the instinct of self-preservation; all public spirit, all generous emotions, all the noble aspirations of man, are shriveling up and disappearing as the volume of primary money shrinks and as prices fall. Honest labor seeks employment it cannot find, and hungry and shelterless, our unemployed are seen daily around the Columbus statue, without hope and in despair.

COIN'S FINANCIAL SCHOOL.

CHAPTER I.

So much uncertainty prevailing about the many facts connected with the monetary question, very few are able to intelligently understand the subject.

Hard times are with us; the country is distracted; very few things are marketable at a price above the cost of production; tens of thousands are out of employment; the jails, penitentiaries, workhouses and insane asylums are full; the gold reserve at Washington is sinking; the government is running at a loss with a deficit in every department; a huge debt hangs like an appalling cloud over the country; taxes have assumed the importance of a mortgage, and 50 per cent of the public revenues are likely to go delinquent; hungered and half-starved men are banding into armies and marching toward Washington; the cry of distress is heard on every hand; business is paralyzed; commerce is at a standstill; riots and strikes prevail throughout the land; schemes to remedy our ills when put into execution are smashed like box-cars in a railroad wreck, and Wall street looks in vain for an excuse to account for the failure of prosperity to return since the repeal of the silver purchase act.

It is a time for wisdom and sound sense to take the helm, and COIN, a young financier living in Chicago, acting upon such a suggestion, established a school of finance to instruct the youths of the nation, with a view to their having a clear understanding of what has been considered an abstruse subject; to lead them out of the labyrinth of falsehoods, heresies and isms that distract the country.

THE FIRST DAY.

COIN ADDRESSES THE SCHOOL

The school opened on the 7th day of May, 1894.

There was a good attendance, and the large hall selected in the Art Institute was comfortably filled. Sons of merchants and bankers, in fact all classes of business, were well represented. Journalists, however, predominated. COIN stepped on to the platform, looking the smooth little financier that he is, and said:

"I am pleased to see such a large attendance. It indicates a desire to learn and master a subject that has baffled your fathers. The reins of the government will soon be placed in your hands, and its future will be molded by your honesty and intelligence.

"I ask you to accept nothing from me that does not stand the analysis of reason; that you will freely ask questions and pass criticisms, and if there is any one present who believes that all who differ from *him* are lunatics and fools, he is requested to vacate his seat and leave the room."

The son of Editor Scott, of the *Chicago Herald*, here arose and walked out. COIN paused a moment, and then continued: "My object will be to teach you the A, B, C of the questions about money that are now a matter of every-day conversation.

THE MONEY UNIT.

"In money there must be a unit. In arithmetic, as you are aware, you are taught what a unit is. Thus, I make here on the blackboard the figure 1. That, in arithmetic, is a unit. All countings are sums or multiples of that unit. A unit, therefore, in mathematics, was a necessity as a basis to start from. In making money it was equally as necessary to establish a unit. The constitution gave the power to Congress to 'coin money and regulate the value thereof.' Congress adopted silver and gold as money. It then proceeded to fix the unit.

"That is, it then fixed what should constitute one dollar, the same thing that the mathematician did when he fixed one figure from which all others should be counted. Congress fixed the monetary unit to consist of 371¼ grains of pure silver, and provided for a certain

THE UNIT IN MATHEMATICS.

amount of alloy (baser metals) to be mixed with it to give it greater hardness and durability. This was in 1792, in the days of Washington and Jefferson and our revolutionary forefathers, who had a hatred of England,

and an intimate knowledge of her designs on this country.

"They had fought eight long years for their independence from British domination in this country, and when they had seen the last red-coat leave our shores, they settled down to establish a permanent government, and among the first things they did was to make 371¼ grains of silver the unit of values. That much silver was to constitute a dollar. And each dollar was a unit. They then provided for all other money to be counted from this unit of a silver dollar. Hence, dimes, quarters and half-dollars were exact fractional parts of the dollar so fixed.

"Gold was made money, but its value was counted from these silver units or dollars. The ratio between silver and gold was fixed at 15 to 1, and afterward at 16 to 1. So that in making gold coins their relative weight was regulated by this ratio.

"This continued to be the law up to 1873. During that long period, the unit of values was never changed and always contained 371¼ grains of pure silver. While that was the law it was impossible for any one to say that the silver in a silver dollar was only worth 47 cents, or any other number of cents less than 100 cents, or a dollar. For it was itself the unit of values. While that was the law it would have been as absurd to say that the silver in a silver dollar was only worth 47 cents, as it would be to say that this figure 1 which I have on the blackboard is only forty-seven one-hundredths of one.

"When the ratio was changed from 15 to 1 to 16 to 1 the silver dollar or unit was left the same size and the gold dollar was made smaller. The latter was changed from 24.7 grains to 23.2 grains pure gold, thus making it smaller. This occurred in 1834. The silver dollar still remained the unit and continued so until 1873.

"Both were legal tender in the payment of all debts, and the mints were open to the coinage of all that came. So that up to 1873, we were on what was known as a bimetallic basis, but what was in fact a silver basis, with gold as a companion metal enjoying the same privileges as silver, except that silver fixed the unit, and the value of gold was regulated by it. This was bimetallism.

"Our forefathers showed much wisdom in selecting silver, of the two metals, out of which to make the unit. Much depended on this decision. For the one selected to represent the unit would thereafter be unchangeable in value. That is, the metal in it could never be worth less than a dollar, for it would be the unit of value itself. The demand for silver in the arts or for money by other nations might make the quantity of silver in a silver dollar sell for more than a dollar, but it could never be worth less than a dollar. Less than itself.

"In considering which of these two metals they would thus favor by making it the unit, they were led to adopt silver because it was the most reliable. It was the most favored as money by the people. It was scattered among all the people. Men having a design to injure business by making money scarce, could not so easily get hold of all the silver and hide it away, as they could gold. This was the principal reason that led them to the conclusion to select silver, the more stable of the two metals, upon which to fix the unit. It was so much handled by the people and preferred by them, that it was called the people's money.

"Gold was considered the money of the rich. It was owned principally by that class of people, and the poor people seldom handled it, and the very poor people seldom ever saw any of it."

THE FIRST INTERRUPTION.

Here young Medill, of the *Chicago Tribune*, held up his hand, which indicated that he had something to say or wished to ask a question. COIN paused and asked him what he wanted.

He arose in his seat and said that his father claimed that we had been on a gold basis ever since 1837, that prior to 1873 there never had been but eight million dollars of silver coined. Here young Wilson, of the *Farm, Field and Fireside*, said he wanted to ask, who owns the *Chicago Tribune?*

COIN tapped the little bell on the table to restore order, and ruled the last question out, as there was one already before the house by Mr. Medill.

"Prior to 1873," said COIN, "there were one hundred and five millions of silver coined by the United States and eight million of this was in silver dollars. When your father said that 'only eight million dollars in silver' had been coined, he meant to say that 'only eight million silver dollars had been coined.' He also neglected to say—that is—he forgot to state, that ninety-seven millions had been coined into dimes, quarters and halves.

"About one hundred millions of foreign silver had found its way into this country prior to 1860. It was principally Spanish, Mexican and Canadian coin. It had all been made legal tender in the United States by act of Congress. We needed more silver than we had, and Congress passed laws making all foreign silver coins legal tender in this country. I will read you one of these laws—they are scattered all through the statutes prior to 1873." Here COIN picked up a copy of the laws of the

United States relating to loans and the currency, coinage and banking, published at Washington. He said: "A copy could be obtained by any one on writing to the Treasury Department."

He then read from page 240, as follows:

"*And be it further enacted*, That from and after the passage of this act, the following foreign silver coins shall pass current as money within the United States, and be receivable by tale, for the payment of all debts and demands, at the rates following, that is to say: the Spanish pillar dollars, and the dollars of Mexico, Peru and Bolivia, etc. * * * * *

"On account of the scarcity of silver, both Jefferson and Jackson recommended that dimes, quarters and halves would serve the people better than dollars, until more silver bullion could be obtained. This was the reason why only about eight million of the one hundred and five million of silver were coined into dollars.

"During this struggle to get more silver," continued COIN, "France made a bid for it by establishing a ratio of 15½ to 1, and as our ratio was 16 to 1, this made silver in France worth $1.03⅛ when exchanged for gold, and as gold would answer the same purpose as silver for money, it was found that our silver was leaving us. So Congress in 1853, had our fractional silver coins made of light weight to prevent their being exported.

"So that we had prior to 1873 one hundred and five millions of silver coined by us, and about one hundred million of foreign silver coin, or about two hundred and five million dollars in silver in the United States, and were doing all we could to get more and to hold on to what we had. Thus silver and gold were the measure of values. It should be remembered that no silver or gold was in circulation between 1860 and 1873. Two hundred and five millions were in circulation before 1861."

Then looking at young Medill, COIN asked him if he had answered his question. The young journalist turned red in the face and hung his head, while young Wilson muttered something about Englishmen owning the *Tribune*.

YOUNG SCOTT RETURNS.

Young Scott was seen entering the room; he was carrying in his hand a book. He stopped and addressed COIN, saying that he wished to apologize for his conduct, and was now here to stay if permitted to do so.

COIN told him that so long as he accorded to others the right to entertain views different from his, his name would be kept on the roll as a student at the "Financial School."

Thereupon Mr. Scott said: "I am informed that you have stated that silver was the unit of value prior to 1873; that this unit was composed of 371¼ grains of pure silver or 412 grains of standard silver. Now I want to know if it is not a fact that both gold and silver at that time were each the unit in its own measurement? And that we had a double measurement of values, which was liable to separate and part company at any time? And when the metals did separate, was not the effect like having two yard-sticks of different lengths? I wish to call your attention to the statute on page 213 of the book you read from where it says an eagle or ten-dollar gold piece is ten *units*. Does not this indicate positively that a gold unit was also provided for?"

And with this he sat down looking as proud as a cannoneer who has just fired a shot that has had deadly effect in the enemy's ranks.

COIN had nodded when the proposition of the *unit*

was stated; looked amused at the double unit proposition advanced, and now replied: "The law I referred to this morning was passed April 2, 1792, and remained the law till 1873. You will find it in my valuable Handbook. I now read it from the United States Statutes:

"*Dollars or units*, each to be of the value of a Spanish milled dollar as the same is now current, and to contain three hundred and seventy-one grains and four-sixteenth parts of a grain of pure, or four hundred and sixteen grains of standard silver.

"If you omit the words referring to the Spanish milled dollar, it will then read: '*Dollars or units, each to contain 371 grains and 4-16 parts of a grain of pure silver.*'

"This is the statute that fixed the *unit* and is the only statute on the subject till we come to 1873.

"Now, what you referred to is this. It is in section 9, and reads as follows:

"*Eagles*—each to be of the *value of* ten dollars or units."

"And on the ratio of 15 to 1, fixed in the same act, this made an eagle contain 247 grains of pure gold, or 270 grains of standard gold. You will observe that the law does not say, as you stated, that an 'Eagle or ten-dollar gold piece *is* ten units.' It says: '*Of the value of ten dollars or units.*' In other words, a ten-dollar gold piece shall *be of the value of ten silver dollars.*

"Or to state it in another way: As the law fixed 371¼ grains of pure silver as a unit, the quantity of gold in a gold dollar would be regulated by the ratio fixed from time to time.

"Now," addressing Mr. Scott, "if I have not read your law right, I want you to say so. This is the place to settle all questions of fact. Your law does not say a gold piece has so many *units* in it, but instead of that, it does say, the gold pieces are *to be of the value* of so many *units*."

The young journalist from Washington street had not seen the distinction, and had jumped at conclusions.

HOW EVANS GOT HIS POLITICAL ECONOMY

When he did see the hole he was in, he leaned over to Evans of the *Economist*, who sat next to him, and asked him to help him out. Evans thought he had mastered the subject of political economy several years ago, and had named his paper "*The Economist*." He found now, that he had not gone very deep into the subject. His text-books had been the *Tribune*, *Herald*, *Record* and *Journal*. He did not know that they, too, were getting their information in about the same way.

So now when his friend Scott was in trouble, he greatly sympathized with him. But he could not help him, and was seen to shake his head. Scott sat silently in his seat.

"You will observe," continued COIN, "that the law in fixing a *dollar* or *unit* does not say, as in the case of gold, that it shall be of the value of 371¼ grains of silver, but that the *dollar* or *unit* was *silver* and its quantity should be 371¼ grains. The amount of alloy added to this quantity of pure silver was afterward changed, but this amount of pure silver, 371¼ grains, has always remained the same and was the unit of values until 1873."

A bright looking kid was now seen standing on a chair in the back part of the room holding up his hand and cracking his finger and thumb. He was asked what he wanted and said:

"I want to know what is meant by *standard* silver?" COIN then explained that this meant with the government a standard rule for mixing alloy with silver and gold. And when so mixed is called standard silver or standard gold. Before it is mixed with the alloy it is called pure silver or pure gold. The standard of both gold and silver is such that by 1,000 parts by weight, 900 shall be of pure metal, and 100 of alloy. The alloy of silver coins is copper. In gold coins it is copper and silver, but the silver shall in no case exceed one-tenth of the whole alloy. Standard silver and standard gold is the metal when mixed with its alloy.

"I now think we understand," said COIN, "what

the unit of value was prior to 1873. We had the silver dollar as the unit. And we had both gold and silver as money walking arm in arm into the United States mints.

THEY WALKED ARM IN ARM INTO THE UNITED STATES MINT.

THE CRIME OF 1873.

"We now come to the act of 1873," continued COIN. "On February 12, 1873, Congress passed an act purporting to be a revision of the coinage laws. This law covers 15 pages of our statutes. It repealed the *unit* clause in the law of 1792, and in its place substituted a law in the following language:

"That the gold coins of the United States shall be a one-dollar piece which at the standard weight of twenty-five and eight-tenths grains *shall be the unit of value.*

"It then deprived silver of its right to unrestricted free coinage, and destroyed it as legal tender money in the payment of debts, except to the amount of five dollars.

"At that time we were all using paper money. No one was handling silver and gold coins. It was when specie payments were about to be resumed that the country appeared to realize what had been done. The newspapers on the morning of February 13, 1873, and at no time in the vicinity of that period, had any account of the change. General Grant, who was President of the United States at that time, said afterwards, that he had no idea of it, and would not have signed the bill if he had known that it demonetized silver.

"In the language of Senator Daniel of Virginia, it seems to have gone through Congress 'like the silent tread of a cat.'

"An army of a half million of men invading our shores, the warships of the world bombarding our coasts, could not have made us surrender the money of the people and substitute in its place the money of the rich. A few words embraced in fifteen pages of statutes put through Congress in the rush of bills did it. The pen was mightier than the sword.

"But we are not here to deal with sentiment. We are here to learn facts. Plain, blunt facts.

"The law of 1873 made gold the *unit* of values. And that is the law to-day. When silver was the unit of value, gold enjoyed *free coinage*, and was legal tender in the payment of all debts. Now things have changed. Gold is the unit and silver does not enjoy free coinage.

THE PEN MORE POWERFUL THAN THE SWORD.

It is refused at the mints. We might get along with gold as the *unit*, if silver enjoyed the same right gold did prior to 1873. But that right is now denied to silver. When silver was the unit, the unlimited demand for gold to coin into money, made the demand as great as the supply, and this held up the value of gold bullion."

Here Victor F. Lawson, Jr., of the Chicago *Evening News*, interrupted the little financier with the statement that his paper, the *News*, had stated time and again that silver had become so plentiful it had ceased to be a precious metal. And that this statement believed by him to be a fact had more to do with his prejudice to silver than anything else. And he would like to know if that was not a fact?

"There is no truth in the statement," replied COIN. "On page 21 of my Handbook you will find a table on this subject, compiled by Mulhall, the London statistician. It gives the quantity of gold and silver in the world both coined and uncoined at six periods—at the years 1600, 1700, 1800, 1848, 1880, and 1890. It shows that in 1600 there were 27 tons of silver to one ton of gold. In 1700, 34 tons of silver to one ton of gold. In 1800, 32 tons of silver to one ton of gold. In 1848, 31 tons of silver to one ton of gold. In 1880, 18 tons of silver to one ton of gold. In 1890, 18 tons of silver to one ton of gold.

"The United States is producing more silver than it ever did, or was until recently. But the balance of the world is producing much less. They are fixing the price on our silver and taking it away from us, at their price. The report of the Director of the Mint shows that since 1850 the world has produced less silver than gold, while during the first fifty years of the century the world produced 78 per cent more silver than gold. Instead of becoming more plentiful, it is less plentiful. So it is less, instead of more.

"Any one can get the official statistics by writing to the treasurer at Washington, and asking for his official book of statistics. Also write to the Director of the Mint and ask him for his report. If you get no answer write to your Congressman. These books are furnished free and you will get them.

HOW SILVER WAS ASSASSINATED.

"At the time the United States demonetized silver in February, 1873, silver as measured in gold was worth $1.02. The argument of depreciated silver could not then be made. Not one of the arguments that are now made against silver was then possible. They are all the bastard children of the crime of 1873.

"It was demonetized secretly, and since then a powerful money trust has used deception and misrepresentations that have led tens of thousands of honest minds astray."

William Henry Smith, Jr., of the Associated Press, wanted to know if the size of the gold dollar was ever changed more than the one time mentioned by COIN, viz., in 1834.

"Yes," said COIN. "In 1837 it was changed from 23.2 to 23.22. This change of $\frac{2}{100}$ths was for convenience in calculation, but the change was made in the gold coin—never in the silver dollar (the *unit*) till 1873.

Adjourned.

BIMETALISM, 1872
FACTORY
SHOP
HOME
SILVER
TAKE YOUR CHOICE
COIN
THIS FACTORY IS CLOSED ON ACCOUNT OF A LACK OF FUNDS
FACTORY
CLOSED
MONOMETALISM, 1894

CHAPTER II.

The Second Day.

When the news went out in Chicago at the end of the first day, that Coin, the little financier, had answered satisfactorily all questions that had been asked him, the old gold men hooted at it, and said that no one but boys were there to confront him.

The morning papers except *The Times* and *Inter Ocean* published a garbled account of what had actually taken place. *The Tribune* and *Herald* were editorially loaded with abuse.

The editor-in-chief of *The Tribune* was a Mr. Van Benthuysen. He had been told by the owners of that paper to write an argument in favor of the gold standard. In an editorial of thirty lines he called bimetallists "fraudulent free silverites," "blatant orators," "blatherskites," "thieves," "swindlers," "repudiators," "dishonest, trickey, brazen charlatans," "malignant lunatics," repeating some of these choice epithets several times.

The next day one of the proprietors called his attention to this editorial and asked him why he did'nt write an argument. His reply was: "Argument! that's the only argument there is!"

On the morning of the second day when Coin arrived at the Art Institute, he found the hall full of people, most of them middle-aged and old men.

He was asked to throw the "school" open to persons of all ages. This was a move to put a quietus on the success of the lectures. Knotty questions would be hurled at him—perplexing queries and abstruse proposi-

THE TRIBUNE MAKES AN ARGUMENT.

tions. They would harass him, worry him, and tangle him, laugh at his dilemma and then say: "We told you so." This was the programme.

COIN consented.

All the seats were filled and many persons were standing. Perfect order prevailed as COIN began his lecture.

THE RATIO.

"The ratio between silver and gold," said COIN, "prior to 1873, in the United States was fixed at 16 to 1, and for the purposes of coining token silver dollars is still the ratio. That is, the silver in a silver dollar is just sixteen times as heavy as the gold in a gold dollar. Or to reverse it, the gold in a gold dollar is just $\frac{1}{16}$th the weight of the silver in a silver dollar.

"Up to 1834, when the ratio was 15 to 1, the gold in a gold dollar was $\frac{1}{15}$th the weight of the silver in a silver dollar. When the ratio was changed to 16 to 1, the quantity of gold in the gold dollar was lessened and made $\frac{1}{16}$th the weight of the silver in a silver dollar.

"The quantity of silver in the silver dollar was not disturbed. It being the unit, was respected, and remained the same. The gold dollar was cut down from 24.7 grains pure gold to 23.2 grains of pure gold. So that now it is one-sixteenth the weight of the pure silver (371¼ grains) in the silver dollar. This is what *ratio* means."

Mr. Lyman Gage, president of the First National Bank of Chicago, interrupted the little speaker.

He had been watching for an opening, and he now thought he had it, where he could deliver a telling, and follow it up with a knock-out, blow.

He rose to his feet. All eyes were on him. In Chicago Lyman Gage is at the "top of the heap." His word is law on the subject of finance. "How does he happen to be at the head of the largest bank west of the Alleghanies, if he does not know all about it?"

This is the way the Chicago people reason when their thinkers are allowed to think.

As a rule they are a very busy set of men. On all such questions as a National finance policy their "thinkers" run automatically. Such men as Mr. Gage do their thinking for them. Cities do not breed statesmen. They breed the specialist. A specialist favors what will

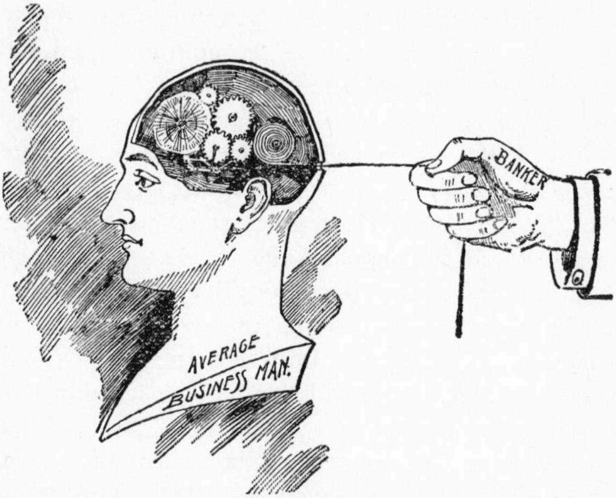

tend to promote his business though it may injure the business of others. A statesman must be broad. He must have a comprehensive appreciation of the interests of all the people—especially the poorer classes. If he has been a railsplitter at one time, so much the better.

The men who produce the property of the world are the men whose happiness should be consulted. The men who handle this property after it is produced have little regard for the interests of the producers. Their selfishness and greed blind them. Their minds are running in a groove and they cannot see the rights of others.

Hence, Mr. Gage is a good banker—a specialist—but a poor statesman. Lincoln was a good statesman, but would have made a poor banker.

The audience was mostly in sympathy with Mr. Gage, except those who had been won over to COIN the day before.

"I would like to ask a question," said Mr. Gage.

"Proceed," said COIN.

"How can you have, at any fixed ratio, the same commercial value on two separate metals, that are from time to time varying in the quantity of each produced?"

"This is the 'stock fallacy' of the gold monometallists," said COIN. "All commercial values are regulated by supply and demand. The commercial value of any commodity depends on supply and demand. If the demand for a particular commodity is continuously rising and the supply does not increase, the *commercial* value will continuously rise.

"When the mints of the world are thrown open and the governments say, 'We will take all the silver and gold that comes,' an *unlimited demand* is established. The supply is limited. Now with an unlimited demand and a limited supply, there is nothing to stop the *commercial* value of the two metals going up in the market, except the governments saying—'Hold on—these metals are for money—we fix the value at which they circulate. This unlimited demand is for silver at $1 for 371¼ grains, and $1 for 23 2-10 grains of gold—we stamp these into dollars respectively in those quantities.'

"While an unlimited demand has been established, the point at which the supply can take advantage of that demand is fixed. And the demand pulls them both plumb up to that point. At 16 to 1 and 371¼ grains of silver as the *unit*, the commercial value of 371 1/4 grains of pure silver is a dollar, and an ounce of silver is worth $1.29 29-100, and 23 2-10 grains of gold is worth a dollar, and an ounce of gold would be worth $20.68 64-100.

"I will illustrate it," and as COIN said this he quickly drew on the blackboard behind him the picture of two hands each drawing a cord through a hole in a beam of wood with blocks on the ends of the cords.

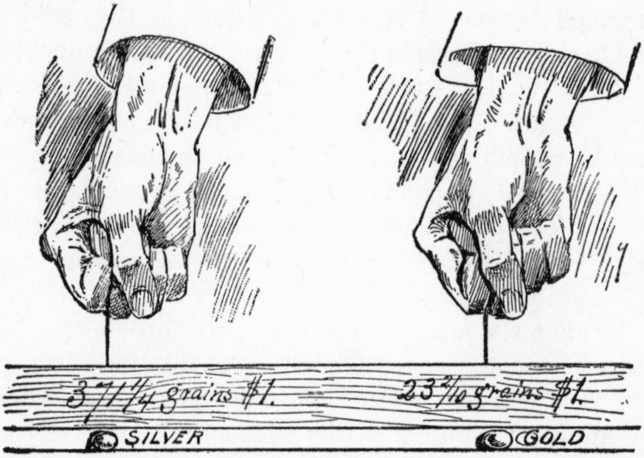

"Now," said COIN, as he leaned over and borrowed from Mr. Owen F. Aldis his cane, and pointing at the drawing on the blackboard, continued: "The hand drawing on the cord represents the power of unlimited demand—the beam represents the price at which the demand stops—and the two little blocks on the ends of the cords, as close up against the beam as they can get, represent silver and gold.

The demand is represented by the two hands; if the one on the silver cord should relax its pull, the little wood block representing silver would drop down. The unlimited demand for one metal (silver) was taken away —the unlimited demand for the other metal (gold) was continued. The whole disturbance since then has come from the demand being taken away from silver."

Mr. Gage had remained standing for a time, then resumed his seat, and became interested.

COIN continuing, said:

"England demonetized silver in 1816, but as Germany, France and the Latin Union, and the United States had their mints open to the free coinage of silver and gold, the demand thus created was sufficient to maintain the parity (equal value) of the two metals, and the action of England had no effect on the price of silver.

"No one in England would part with his silver for less than an equal value in gold, when he could cross the channel into France and get an even exchange—so the price of silver as measured in gold was during all the years prior to 1873 substantially at par in England and the world over.

"The United States closed its mints to silver and made gold the sole measurement of values in February, 1873.

"Germany followed and passed the same law in July, 1873. The action of these two large nations caused a drop in the commercial value of silver as measured in gold of 2 per cent by the end of that year.

"France and the Latin Union closed their mints to the free coinage of silver in January, 1874, and by the end of that year silver as measured in gold had declined 4 per cent.

"Then came the gradual breaking down of the commercial price of silver as measured in the new standard —gold—and acts were passed tending to this end. Among them were the acts of 1876 stopping the coinage of the trade dollars by which we were supplying China and the Orient with coin, and the law in 1878 authorizing and sanctioning notes, bonds and mortgages, to be taken payable in *gold only*. This latter is a clause in the Bland-Allison act, a copy of which can be found in Coin's Hand Book, or can be obtained from any of your congressmen. It discriminates against all our other forms of money and [illegible] the creditor to dictate that his credits shall be payable in *gold*.

"These acts have been followed up by the declared policy of the government to redeem all other money, including silver, in gold.

"The same class of legislation was simultaneously in progress in Europe, so that by the summer of 1893 silver had declined 35 per cent. Then came the closing of the mints of India to silver and the decline increased to 50 per cent.

THEIR COMMERCIAL VALUES COMPARED.

"Comparing the prices," continued Coin, "of the relative commercial values of the two metals for the whole world, Mr. Sauerbeck, an English statistician, has prepared a table showing the value of silver as measured in gold for 19 years before and 19 years subsequent to 1873. The table expresses it in index numbers. It is London quotations.

"I have these tables printed," said Coin, "and will cause them to be distributed among you."

Little boys then went through the school and gave every one a copy of the table.

Coin waited till the tables were distributed and then, looking straight at Mr. Gage, he said:

"You will see from this table that during the 19 years prior to 1873, while *free coinage* was the law in the nations I have named, the commercial value of silver in the London market — in gold standard Eng-

MR. SAUERBECK'S TABLE.

Years from 1873 back to 1854.	Yearly Index-numbers of Silver	Yearly Index-numbers of silver	Years from 1873 on to 1892.
1873	97.4	97.4	1873
1872	99.2	95.8	1874
1871	99.7	93.3	1875
1870	99.6	86.7	1876
1869	99.6	90.2	1877
1868	99.6	86.4	1878
1867	99.7	84.2	1879
1866	100.5	85.9	1880
1865	100.3	85.0	1881
1864	100.9	84.9	1882
1863	101.1	83.1	1883
1862	100.9	83.3	1884
1861	99.9	79.9	1885
1860	101.4	74.6	1886
1859	102.0	73.3	1887
1858	101.0	70.4	1888
1857	101.5	70.2	1889
1856	101.0	78.4	1890
1855	100.7	74.1	1891
1854	101.1	65.4	1892

land — did not vary either way more than 2 per cent. — $\frac{8}{10}$ of 1 per cent under was the least, and 2 per cent over was the greatest. The average for the 19 years shows a premium on silver over gold, which is explained by the disturbance created by the difference in ratios in France and the United States.

"If the same ratio had existed in all these countries, then the only difference would have been the exchange difference, the cost of freight in the movement of bullion when unevenly distributed as between silver and gold when needed at different points.

"Nor did the varying quantities of silver and gold in the world, during this period from 1854 to 1872, have the least effect on the relative commercial value of the two metals.

"Mr. Mulhall, the London Statistician, has compiled statistics showing the relative quantity of silver and gold in the world at different periods, and his figures are substantiated by the official reports of the governments of the world from which they were taken.

"He gives the relative quantity in 1848, 1880 and 1890, but does not give it at any other date between these periods. But taking the dates he does give, we find that in 1848 there were 31 tons of silver to 1 ton of gold in the world. In 1880, 18 tons of silver to 1 ton of gold. In 1890, 18 tons of silver to 1 ton of gold.

"Now as the relative supply of silver to gold was decreasing from 1848 to 1880, then this decrease was in progress between 1854 and 1872, and yet during this period it had no effect on the relative value of the two metals.

"If Mr. Sauerbeck's table was extended back to 1848 or to 1792, the variation in it would be no greater than existed between 1854 to 1872.

"And yet we find that there were 31 tons of silver in 1848 to 1 ton of gold — a large over-production of silver as compared with gold. Using the official figures given by Mr. Mulhall, and estimating from them, the proportion in 1872 was 19 tons of silver to 1 of gold. The production of silver had become materially less as compared with gold, and yet through all these years from 1848 to 1872, there was no difference in the commercial value of the two metals that would not be accounted for by the French ratio disturbance and the cost of exchanging the two metals.

"During the period between 1849 and 1854 the gold mines of California added largely to the world's stock of gold. So much so that men of Mr. Gage's views as to supply of the two metals varying, started a propaganda for the demonetization of gold.

"And yet with all that gold output, we find that it had no effect on the relative commercial values of the two metals. The reason why it could have had no effect was because the demand for either was unlimited. Both enjoyed the same advantage in that respect.*

The attempt that was then made to demonetize gold had not gone far, when to the surprise of those that were engaged in it, gold maintained its commercial value. They realized then by the practical workings of *free coinage* of the two metals, their error and abandoned the effort.

"Had specie payments been in operation in 1873, no doubt silver never would have been demonetized. Nearly every one would have been alive to the interest of our metallic money and it would have been daily asserting its own importance as in 1850–54.

"It was during a period of suspension of specie payments in England following the French war that parlament demonetized silver in 1816, in much the same manner that it was accomplished in this country.

A COMPARISON FOR 200 YEARS.

"To show you how perfectly the law of free coinage worked from time immemorial till 1873, in sustaining the *commercial* value of silver and gold at a parity, I am now going to distribute among you a copy of page 50 of the 'Statistical Abstract' for 1892, issued by the Treasury Department of the United States."

Coin waited until they were distributed, and every one in the room had one in his hand, including Mr. Gage.

---

*See world's production 1852-3-4, Coin's Hand Book, p. 26.

(Page 50 from U. S. Statistical Abstract 1892.)

RATIO OF SILVER TO GOLD.

COMMERCIAL RATIO OF SILVER TO GOLD FOR EACH YEAR SINCE 1687.

[NOTE.—From 1687 to 1832 the ratios are taken from the tables of Dr. A. Soetbeer; from 1833 to 1878 from Pixley and Abell's tables; and from 1878 to 1892 from daily cablegrams from London to the Bureau of the Mint.]

Year.	Ratio.	Year.	Ratio	Year.	Ratio.	Year.	Ratio.	Year.	Ratio.	Year.	Ratio.
1687	14.94	1722	15.17	1757	14.87	1791	15.05	1825	15.70	1859	15.19
1688	14.94	1723	15.20	1758	14.85	1792	15.17	1826	15.76	1860	15.29
1689	15.02	1724	15.11	1759	14.15	1793	15.00	1827	15.74	1861	15.50
1690	15.02	1725	15.11	1760	14.14	1794	15.37	1828	15.78	1862	15.35
1691	14.98	1726	15.15	1761	14.54	1795	15.55	1829	15.78	1863	15.37
1692	14.92	1727	15.24	1762	15.27	1796	15.65	1830	15.82	1864	15.37
1693	14.83	1728	15.11	1763	14.99	1797	15.41	1831	15.72	1865	15.44
1694	14.87	1729	14.92	1764	14.70	1798	15.59	1832	15.73	1866	15.43
1695	15.02	1730	14.81	1765	14.83	1799	15.74	1833	15.93	1867	15.57
1696	15.00	1731	14.94	1766	14.80	1800	15.68	1834	15.73	1868	15.59
1697	15.20	1732	15.09	1767	14.85	1801	15.46	1835	15.80	1869	15.60
1698	15.07	1733	15.18	1768	14.80	1802	15.26	1836	15.72	1870	15.57
1699	14.94	1734	15.39	1769	14.72	1803	15.41	1837	15.83	1871	15.57
1700	14.81	1735	15.41	1770	14.62	1804	15.41	1838	15.85	1872	15.63
1701	15.07	1736	15.18	1771	14.66	1805	15.79	1839	15.62	1873	15.92
1702	15.52	1737	15.02	1772	14.52	1806	15.52	1840	15.62	1874	**16.17**
1703	15.17	1738	14.91	1773	14.62	1807	15.43	1841	15.70	1875	**16.59**
1704	15.22	1739	14.91	1774	14.62	1808	16.08	1842	15.87	1876	**17.88**
1705	15.11	1740	14.94	1775	14.72	1809	15.96	1843	15.93	1877	**17.22**
1706	15.27	1741	14.92	1776	14.55	1810	15.77	1844	15.85	1878	**17.94**
1707	15.44	1742	14.85	1777	14.54	1811	15.53	1845	15.92	1879	**18.40**
1708	15.41	1743	14.85	1778	14.68	1812	16.11	1846	15.90	1880	**18.05**
1709	15.31	1744	14.87	1779	14.80	1813	16.25	1847	15.80	1881	**18.16**
1710	15.22	1745	14.98	1780	14.72	1814	15.04	1848	15.85	1882	**18.19**
1711	15.29	1746	15.13	1781	14.78	1815	15.26	1849	15.78	1883	**18.64**
1712	15.31	1747	15.26	1782	14.42	1816	15.28	1850	15.70	1884	**18.57**
1713	15.24	1748	15.11	1783	14.48	1817	15.11	1851	15.46	1885	**19.41**
1714	15.13	1749	14.80	1784	14.70	1818	15.35	1852	15.59	1886	**20.78**
1715	15.11	1750	14.55	1785	14.92	1819	15.33	1853	15.33	1887	**21.13**
1716	15.09	1751	14.39	1786	14.96	1820	15.62	1854	15.33	1888	**21.99**
1717	15.13	1752	14.54	1787	14.92	1821	15.95	1855	15.38	1889	**22.09**
1718	15.11	1753	14.54	1788	14.65	1822	15.80	1856	15.38	1890	**19.75**
1719	15.09	1754	14.48	1789	14.75	1823	15.84	1857	15.27	1891	**20.92**
1720	15.04	1755	14.68	1790	15.04	1824	15.82	1858	15.38	1892	**23.72**
1721	15.05	1756	14.94								

DEMONETIZATION.

"You will see from this table," continued COIN, "that from 1687 to 1873 the *commercial* ratio of the two metals was never lower than 1 to 14.14, and never higher than 1 to 16.25, a variation of only about two points.

"This difference is accounted for by the difference in ratios fixed by different governments, and the cost of exchange; ours being 15 to 1 prior to 1834.

"Run your eyes down these columns from 1687 to 1873 and see how smooth the *commercial* ratio appears.

"Now *all stop*, with your fingers on 1873! Up to this point through two centuries we see how the commercial value of silver and gold was kept at a parity notwithstanding the varying supplies of the two metals.

"Now run your fingers down from 1873 to 1892, and in that short period what a change, O! my countrymen.

"Instead of 15 to 16 pounds of silver being worth one pound of gold, we see it jumping rapidly, till in 1892 it took nearly 24 pounds of silver to equal in commercial value one pound of gold. And now it takes *32 pounds* of silver to equal in the market *one pound* of gold.

"While in 200 years there was under *free coinage* a variation of only about 2 points, in 21 years, under demonetization there is a variation of 16 points, and during the latter period the proportion of silver to gold produced has been growing less.

We here have a demonstration of how free coinage controls the *commercial* value of the two metals.

"So true and accurate was this effect of free coinage or *unlimited demand* for both metals in fixing their parity at the ratio established, they were virtually one metal, and a difference in production of either could not have, and did not have, the least influence.

"I will illustrate it another way." In less than a minute COIN had drawn on the blackboard two reservoirs filled with water and connected with each other by a pipe.

"Now," said COIN, pointing with the cane at the reservoirs and their connecting pipe, "the water in one of these reservoirs represents silver and the other gold. The connecting pipe makes them virtually one metal and either answers the requirement of the government

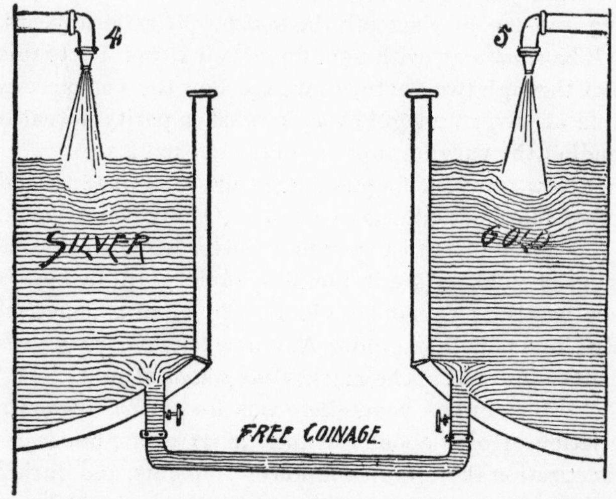

for money. So long as that connecting pipe remains, the water in the two reservoirs will remain even—the same height. Do away with the connecting pipe and the feed pipes at 4 and 5 will soon destroy the equilibrium, as their quantities vary from time to time.

"The law of free coinage (the connecting pipe) maintains the parity of the two metals. When that was taken away from silver and left on gold a disturbance was natural.

"Prior to 1873, when the *connecting pipe* was working freely, the ratio in France was 15½ to 1, while in this country it was 16 to 1, and this difference in ratio was the only disturbing element, causing only slight fluctuations in the comparative value of the two metals, when measured in each other—this depending on the direction in which the bullion was moving.

"But the moment the 'connecting pipe' was cut, the derangement in the values of the metals and *of all property* began.

"And now," said COIN, "if I have not answered Mr. Gage's question, I want him to say why I have not."

COIN had been listened to with rapt attention. A pin could almost have been heard to drop at any moment. No sound was heard except the voice of the young speaker, whose pleasant style of address had a charm about it that did not wear away.

There were many scholars and thoughtful business men in the audience—men of intelligence. Many of them owned large business blocks. Capitalists who had made Chicago what it is—such men as Leander McCormick, H. H. Kohlsaat, L. Z. Leiter, Phil. D. Armour, Potter Palmer and Samuel Allerton; merchant princes like Marshall Field, John V. Farwell and Franklin MacVeagh; lawyers of local and national reputation, such as Luther Laflin Mills, Judge Henry G. Miller, Judge Collins, Jno. S. Cooper, Edwin Walker and A. S. Trude.

There was a fascination in COIN'S manner of delivery that had caused every word he uttered to be heard and understood. They had listened critically, expecting to detect errors in his facts or reasoning. There were none. They were amazed. He was logical.

Real estate owners who had seen their rents going down, their houses becoming vacant, while their taxes were growing bigger; merchants who had been doing business on a falling market for twenty years, now felt as if they had each an interest in this money question.

MR. GAGE MAKES AN ADMISSION.

Mr. Gage arose and said:

"What you have said about the commercial value of silver and gold being maintained at a parity under a fixed ratio, has been due to the enlarged use of these two metals, as money, under a free coinage law adopted by the principal nations of the world. International bimetallism would do what you say. But the United States alone could not maintain the parity of the two metals. Silver would be the cheaper, and gold would leave us. We would have no credit abroad, and a total derangement of our commerce would follow. And in this respect you have not satisfactorily answered my question."

"Then, Mr. Gage," said COIN, "we agree, do we, that the commercial value of silver and gold can be maintained at par on a fixed ratio at 15½ to 1 or 16 to 1, if their free coinage is provided for by the same nations that had such a law in 1873?"

"Yes," said Mr. Gage, "we agree thus far."

"Thanks," said COIN. "If all are as well satisfied thus far as Mr. Gage, we have gained a great deal. To understand these fundamental principles as far as we have gone, and as adapted and applied in the past, and as tested and proven a success, is essential to our further study of this subject.

"In arranging the programme for this school, I thought it best to leave the subject of independent free coinage by the United States to the last. I will not now change the order. When I answer that question it will be as simple and as satisfactory as any we have yet encountered.

"From the tone of the press in this city, it will be readily understood that we do not agree on the cause of the present depression in business, and how much of it is properly chargeable to the demonetization of silver. Let us first find out the cause of this calamitous condition of things and then we will speak of the remedy.

"We have seen that the closing of the mints, first of the United States, secondly Germany in 1873, followed by France and the Latin Union in 1874, depressed the price of silver as measured in gold 35 per cent. And the closing of the mints to silver in India, in 1893, further depressed its price to 50 per cent.

QUANTITY OF GOLD AND SILVER.

"Before demonetization both metals constituted the redemption money of the world; and as both metals existed in about the same quantities, it gave us twice as much money of redemption as gold alone will now furnish us. There is in the world now, according to the report of the director of our mint, $3,727,018,869 in gold, and $3,820,571,346 in silver.

"The dislocation of the parity of the two metals by the demonetization of silver, and the attempt to maintain our credit in gold, has reduced the redemption money of the world from $7,547,590,215 to $3,727,018,869, or a little less than one-half the original amount."

A REAL ESTATE MAN ASKS A QUESTION.

"I want to know," said Mr. George H. Rozet, a real estate dealer, here interrupting COIN, "why you say silver is demonetized, when it is in circulation every day and handled by us as money?"

"We have seen," replied COIN, "how the commercial value of the two metals were parted. By the same laws that produced this result, silver was made redeemable in gold, and ceased to be redemption money. Silver now circulates like paper money, both redeemable in gold. It is now subsidary coin or token money.

"Strictly speaking, nothing is money but redemption money—all other forms of so called money are money only in the sense that certified checks are money.

"In the sense in which *you* say silver is money, nickel and copper are money, but they form no part of our stock of redemption money. Gold now takes the place formerly occupied by both gold and silver, and is our only redemption money. Silver, as now treated, cuts no figure in our currency that could not be substituted by paper or other metals. What is meant by demonetization is, that silver has been destroyed as primary money.

"We are now on a single gold standard, and have come to it through a period of limping bimetallism."

CHANGING RATIO.

Mr. Fred Miller, cashier of the Bank of Commerce, announced a desire to ask a question and proceeded to state it.

"It appears," said Mr. Miller, "that whenever the ratio has been changed, the number of grains of pure silver in the silver dollar has not been disturbed, while the quantity of gold in the gold coin has been changed;

I want to know if there is any particular significance in this? Why change the gold and not the silver?"

"As silver was the *unit*," answered COIN, "more respect was paid to it than to the other metal. But there was another reason that would ordinarily have a controlling influence. I mean the cost of re-coining. There are about one hundred pieces of silver coin to one piece of gold coin. In coining ten million dollars in dimes, it requires the striking off of one hundred million coins. To coin one million dollars in quarters requires the striking off of four million coins. One million dollars in halves requires two million coins. One million silver dollars one million coins.

"While in making our gold money, comparatively few coins are required to be struck. One million dollars in ten dollar gold pieces requires only one hundred thousand pieces to be struck, and in twenties, 50,000. It would be much more expensive to recoin the silver than the gold. It would also be of great inconvenience to the government and the people to gather in all the silver coins, while it is of small inconvenience comparatively to collect in and recoin the gold.

"To re-coin the silver money is more expensive, and would take a much longer time than to re-coin the gold. But the greatest significance is in the fact that it was the money of the people. Its integrity and identity was respected by our forefathers.

"As our time to close the school for the day has arrived, we will now adjourn till 10 o'clock to-morrow morning." (Adjourned.)

Mr. Gage, and all those who, like him, had gone to hear COIN for the purpose of refuting his arguments, walked out of the room in a thoughtful manner.

They had previously reached conclusions that the

gold standard was the proper thing. They had only studied one side of the question. They had become firm in their opinions, and had worked up memorials to Congress against the free coinage of silver.

They had not based these opinions on the necessity of international bimetallism, but upon the theory that a gold standard is the best financial system for the United States to adopt.

Now, having met for the first time some one who knew the science of money, they were surprised. That it should come from the lips of a boy they were more surprised. Instead of scoffing at him, and confusing him, they had listened and been compelled to give assent to his plain and unanswerable views.

Their hope now laid in preventing him from showing that the demonetization of silver was the cause of low prices — stagnation in business, and the deranged industrial condition of the country. That we have been compelled to adopt a financial system forced upon us by Europe.

A POLITICIAN GETS THE WORST OF AN ARGUMENT.

CHAPTER III.

The Third Day.

An increased interest was plainly seen in the large attendance on the third day. Coin was also received with marked favor, and groups gathered around him as he entered the hall and warmly shook his hand.

He was assured that Chicago had many bimetallists, but that the subject had been a perplexing one to the people. It was regarded as an abstruse question, and the people generally had not tried to unravel it. It required the knowledge of so many statistics and facts with which the masses were not familiar, they were hardly expected to understand it.

Mr. Joel Bigelow, of 2449 Prairie avenue, was one of the most demonstrative in a cordial greeting to the little financier.

Give it to them, young man," said Mr. Bigelow. "The eyes of the people here have been blinded with this gold craze. I have been distributing Archbishop Walsh's pamphlet among them and have opened some of their eyes."

Mr. Bigelow is an exception to most bimetallists. He had not been forced by personal business disaster to inquire into the cause of so many failures. He is a large real estate owner, owes no debts and has plenty laid by. He is philanthropic. He believes in the happiness of the people. Would that there were more such men!

With a pleasant salutation to all, COIN moved along through the crowd until he reached the stage, and promptly at 10 o'clock began his lecture of the third day.

"The science of money," he began, "is an exact science. As much so as mathematics.

"The primary value of all property is its exchange value. If we had no money, one kind of property would be exchanged for another. Needing the calico on the merchant's shelf, you would exchange for it a bushel of potatoes or such property as you might have to offer. A sort of exchange value would be placed on all property. A bushel of wheat would buy about so many pounds of sugar, and so on.

"This is what is meant by the exchange value of property. Money is a medium of exchange to facilitate this exchanging of property.

"If there were no money, and we had to depend on exchanging property for property, we could find a subsistence, but there would be no such thing as our present civilization or anything like it.

"Each merchant would have to be prepared to store all kinds of property, perishable and otherwise, he received in exchange for his goods. Railroads would have to arrange to receive payment for fares and freight in property and store it until it again could be exchanged.

"If you went to the theater you would have to take with you a crate of cabbage or some other kind of property to pay your way into the play-house.

"There would be no practical method for paying labor. Commerce would virtually cease, and civilization would go backward.

"If to be without money would produce such a result, then the subject assumes vast importance.

"As stagnation and depression to business incalculable would result from having no money, then a part of these evils can be brought about by having money insufficient in either quality or quantity.

EXCHANGING PROPERTY FOR THEATRE TICKETS.

"In the first place, it was deemed best to select something for money which was valuable within itself. Something that had an exchange value. So that he who parted with his property for it, had something which was itself valuable.

"By stamping it as money, and making it legal tender in the payment of all debts, it then became money, and possessed two qualities:

"First; It had value of itself. If the government went to pieces that had stamped it, it was still valuable property and would have an exchange value.

"Secondly; When made money, it became a common medium of exchange and took the place of barter and trade. The stamp of the government upon it, became a certificate of its quality and quantity. Thus by making a commodity into money we had a medium of exchange that was both useful and valuable.

SILVER AND GOLD ADOPTED.

"After using many perishable commodities, experience and wisdom brought the people of the world to the use of silver and gold.

"If experience could suggest a commodity better adapted for money than metallic money made from silver and gold, it should be adopted.

"The merit of these two metals is that neither will rust, corrode nor stain, and both are odorless. As compared with other property, both are very durable. Of the two, silver is the most durable. Abrasion causes more loss to gold than to silver, and the latter may be carried in the pocket and subjected to great use with but little loss. One was the money of the people—the other, of the rich. As two legs are necessary to walk and two eyes to see, so were these two monies necessary to the prosperity of the people.

SINGLE STANDARD.

SINGLE STANDARD.

"It was considered that silver and gold were sufficient in quantity for use as primary money, but if at any time their combined quantity should become too small, then some other metal would have to be adopted and added to these two. The law of unlimited demand by *free coinage*, would tie a third metal to these two, and thus increase the quantity, if at any time it became necessary.

"Thus the founders of a monetary system, on the principle of *free coinage* to the commodity selected, had a practical method for supplying any deficiency that might arise by reason of the exhaustion of the silver and gold mines."

AN INTERRUPTION

Thus far everyone had listened attentively, and no one had interrupted the little speaker.

Now Mr. John R. Walsh, president of the Chicago National Bank and prinicipal owner of *The Chicago Herald* and *Evening Post*, who occupied a seat near the front, arose and asked this question:

"How can the government by passing a law add a cent to the commercial value of any commodity?"

"You were not here yesterday?" said COIN to Mr. Walsh. To this Mr. Walsh replied that he was not.

"Suppose," said COIN, "that Congress should pass a law to-morrow authorizing the purchase by the government of 100,000 cavalry horses of certain sizes and qualities. And the government entered the market to get these horses. Horses would advance in value. Not only the kind of horses desired, but also other horses upon which there would be a demand to take the place of the horses sold to the government."

SINGLE STANDARD.

The hand-clapping that followed this reply, and smiles on many faces, indicated two things—one was, that the reply was satisfactory; the other, that the school was making progress—for it was the first applause COIN had received.

"The government," continued COIN, "can create a demand for a commodity.

"The prospect of a law being passed will sometimes add to the value of property. The tariff law was recently being considered by the Finance Committee of the Senate, and on its becoming known that the committee would report in favor of a high tariff on sugar, the market value of the stock of the American Sugar Refining Company advanced 15 per cent. Its total stock is eighty million dollars. This prospect of a law passing added twelve millions of dollars to the wealth of the stockholders of that company. If Mr Walsh will read the proceedings of yesterday's school, he will see how free coinage fixes the commercial value of silver.

SINGLE STANDARD.

"In the *free coinage* of silver as money, the effect is not to increase its exchange value, but to give a permanent and fixed value."

MONEY AS A SCIENCE

" We are now dealing with money as a science, and, strictly speaking, nothing is money except that commodity which has been selected to be money. It is a common thing for us to refer to National Bank notes, greenbacks and other forms of paper money as 'money.'

" After a nation has fixed what its *money* shall be, it then issues different forms of credit money all of which are directly or indirectly redeemable in the commodity to which a fixed and stable value has been given.

" This is done for convenience, and to facilitate commerce and the exchange of property. It does not add one dollar to your actual money but represents your real money, and being easier to carry, is a convenience.

"All money may be a medium of exchange, but primary money *only* is the measure of values. Credit money is not a measure of values ; it is a medium of exchange only.

" I will refer to *money* proper as *redemption* or *primary* money, and in speaking generally of all other forms of money, will use the term *credit* money.

"There are two kinds of *credit* money, as to the material out of which they are made. One is made on paper and embraces all forms of government and bank notes that are issued from time to time as authorized by law. The other is—token money.

"Token money is made from some metal that does not enjoy *free coinage.*

" *Credit money* of all kinds circulates by reason of its being redeemable directly or indirectly in *money*—in *redemption* money, property money. A piece of paper money, or token money, is a promise of the government to pay so much money. The money promised is the *redemption* money.

"With so much paper or credit money in your possession, there is supposed to be that much redemption money to your credit with the government or bank issuing it. It is a check to bearer for *money*, when presented.

"Hence it is called *credit* money. It circulates on the credit of the government, on the confidence of the people that the government will be able to redeem it if it is presented.

"I have taken pains to impress on you the distinction between actual money and credit money, as no just comprehension of our monetary system as a science can be had without it.

"Actual money was too cumbersome to handle in all the transactions of business, and this gave rise to issuing credit money representing it. Like wheat in your wheat elevators certificates are issued to those who put their wheat there. Such certificates are traded in. Each time one of them is transferred, it is equivalent to transferring the wheat itself. Wheat is behind the certificates. A man does not carry a brick house around in his pocket, but he can carry the deed to it.

"When you have credit money in your pocket, you are carrying around with you the title to property of that commercial value.

"In issuing dollar for dollar of credit money to redemption money, it is not necessary that the government should keep the latter at all times in its treasury in full amount ready to redeem all the credit money.

"Experience teaches that so long as sufficient *redemption money* is in the country, the credit of the government can be depended upon to get it. But it cannct strain the proportion beyond such amount without making the danger imminent, and the lack of confidence great.

"If there is one thousand million dollars of redemption money in the United States—in its treasury, its banks, and among its people—then one thousand millions of credit money can be safely used and not more.

"If you want to increase the currency, you must in safety do it by adding to the *redemption* money, and for each dollar so added one dollar of credit money may be added.

DIGGING OUT THE FOUNDATION.

"If it is wished to vitiate the currency, increase the credit money beyond its normal quantity, or dig out the foundation from under it by lessening the supply of redemption money.

"The demonetization of silver destroyed one-half of the *redemption* money of the United States. It did it in this way: By making gold the *unit* and closing the mints to silver, it lessened the demand for silver, and its commercial value at once began to depreciate, as measured in gold.

"Where before silver and gold had been tied together as one mass of commodity money, and all property had measured its value in it, now gold became the only measure of value, and silver became *credit* money—token money.

"The moment a new standard of money was set up—only one-half in quantity to what had previously existed—silver began to fluctuate. It was then measured for its value in this new standard for measuring values, and bobbed up and down in the market, no longer possessing that fixed value which *free* coinage had given it. It was like a kite without a tail and its course was downward. It had changed its position from redemption money to token money.

"A forced parity between gold and silver has since been strained; namely, by sustaining silver with gold. It is the same kind of parity the government maintains between gold and paper money. What this means is, gold is our present redemption money and our credit money consists of silver and all forms of paper money.

"Each succeeding secretary of the treasury points to the law declaring it to be the intention of our financial system to maintain all our money at par. Gold is the most valuable of all our money, and therefore to maintain it all at par, gold must stand under it and do the work of redemption money.

"The law simply states an axiom in sound financeering. All of our money should be at par; with one kind of money just as good as any other kind of money.

"It is impossible to maintain two kinds of redemption money with one made from property having a commercial value of only one-half, or any noticeable per cent less than the other. When such is the case the lesser must lean on the greater, and to all intents and purposes becomes credit money, while the more valuable becomes the only redemption money.

"We have in the United States in round figures $1,600,000,000 of all kinds of money. About one-third of it is gold, one-third silver and one-third paper. One-third of our money is redemption money, and two-thirds is credit money.

"The blunder was made when silver was demonetized. The remedy is to remonetize it, and thereby restore its commercial value. Purchase acts, or any treatment of silver short of free coinage will have no beneficial effect."

Mr. D. H. Wheeler wanted to know of COIN if he did not believe it would advance prices if the government were to issue five hundred millions of greenbacks.

"No;" was the reply. "It would break down the present tottering financial system the sooner. The remedy to restore prices, is to remonetize silver, and then issue more greenbacks.

GENERAL PRINCIPLES

"We thus see that *money*, primarily, is a commodity—property—a thing of value—possessing an exchange value with all other property.

"That *credit money* is a title to *commodity money*. That in the exchange value between *commodity money* and all other property, credit money does not add anything—it facilitates—makes convenient the transaction of business. Just as your wheat certificates add nothing to the exchange value of wheat, or the things for which wheat are exchanged ; yet they facilitate its exchange.

"This commodity money is the measure of values. Its quantity becomes the measure, and each dollar is a part of that measure. Credit money adds nothing to its value, it only facilitates the transaction of business based on that measure of values.

"Our commodity or redemption money, up to 1873, was both silver and gold ; and our credit money was paper and copper.

"Since 1873 our redemption money has been gold—and our credit money has been paper, silver, nickel and copper. Silver and nickel have been added to copper as token money."

Here Mr. Walsh arose again, and COIN paused to hear the question he evidently intended to ask.

"Has not," asked Mr. Walsh, "the necessity for money diminished since checks, drafts and bills of exchange have come into such prominent use? The first use of money is to effect exchanges, and as a vast bulk of exchanges, are affected without money, should not this be deducted from the bulk of exchange before a normal amount of money can be considered?"

"That is a statement of common error," said COIN, "and others urge it with as much confidence as Mr. Walsh. That situation does lessen the amount of credit money employed ; but it does not diminish the amount of *redemption* money necessary. Credit money is not used for its value, but for its convenience. Any other convenience which you can substitute for it may be made to answer the same purpose.

"As *redemption money* is our measure of values, nothing can take its place and assist it in *its* work that is not of equal commercial value.

"It is also an error to suppose that checks and drafts to any very great extent take the place of *credit* money. It facilitates business for a man to be able to carry his check book with him instead of the danger and inconvenience of carrying a large roll of bills; but the equivalent of each check he draws must be to his credit in bank to meet the check. If a man gives a check for $100, and that check is transferred to six different parties and pays in that way six different debts in the course of the day, it does no more than a $100 bill would have done. It, too, could have started on the rounds and paid the same number of debts. The check has no advantages over the bill in that respect.

"Where checks enlarge the use of credit money is in this: A bank may have had deposited with it $1,000,000. It only keeps say $400,000 on hand; the banking and check system give greater utility to the $1,000,000, but the necessity for *actual* money has not been decreased in the least—the expansion of credit money by substitutes only emphasizes its importance.

OUR FINANCIAL AND CREDIT SYSTEM

"Three lines of credits," continued COIN, "are built up on *primary* or *redemption* money.

"*First:* Credit money—paper bills and all forms of token money—all redeemable in primary money.

"*Second:* Checks, drafts, bills of exchange, and other forms of like paper, payable on demand.

"*Third:* Notes, bonds, accounts, and other forms of credit, payable at a particular day in the future, or upon the happening of some contingency.

"A reckless era of business that extends either or both the *second* and *third* lines of credit beyond their normal volume may create a panic. Notes, bonds and accounts become due that are not paid; a lack of confidence arises resulting in the demand for all debts due for fear delay will endanger their collection.

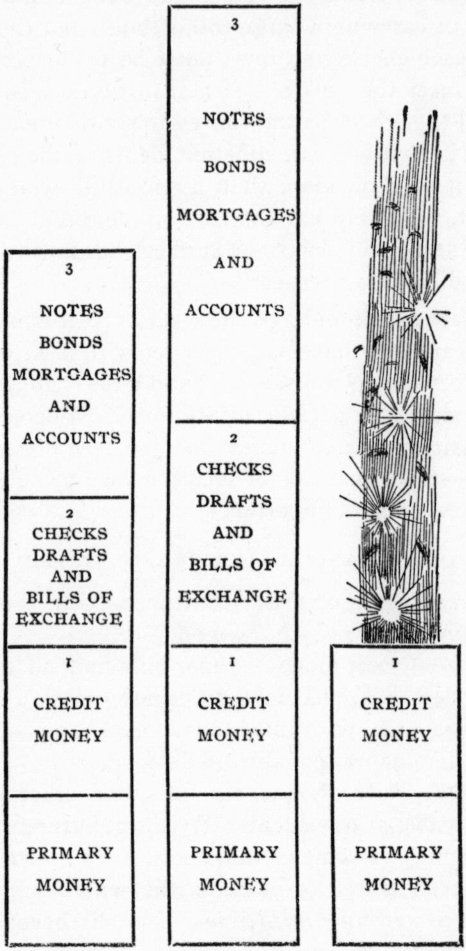

First Lesson. Second Lesson. Third Lesson.

"A run on banks during such a period is natural, and many of them go down for want of sufficient reserve to pay all money deposited with them subject to check.

"I will illustrate it."

As he said this he unrolled a chart, and as he proceeded he disclosed others, illustrating the relation of primary money to credits.

"The base section of these columns," he said, pointing with a stick at the illustrations, "represents *commodity* or *property* money. The next, or second, represents *credit money*. The third represents checks, and all forms of personal credits payable on demand. The fourth represents notes, bonds, mortgages, accounts, and all forms of debts calling for money, made when contracted payable in the future. Thus we have—one—two—three—sections of credit built up on primary money.

"The column marked FIRST LESSON presents a normal or healthy condition of things—a proportion which it would not be safe to greatly alter.

"The column marked SECOND LESSON shows a proportion brought about by over-confidence. It is what often happens when the country is prosperous. A man in ordinary circumstances finds that he can easily float $5,000 dollars in debts; and as his business is prosperous, he increases it to $10,000. This expansion becomes contagious. Cities, counties, corporations—all increase their debts.

"The column marked THIRD LESSON shows the result this condition produces.

"In this instance which I have illustrated, the fault, or cause of the panic, has been entirely with the second and third columns of credit. Primary money and the first column—*credit money*—have not been at fault. Such panics are not of long duration.

"I now call your attention to the FOURTH LESSON, where the first, second and third sections of credit are all expanded beyond their proportion to primary money.

"The FIFTH LESSON shows the result this produces.

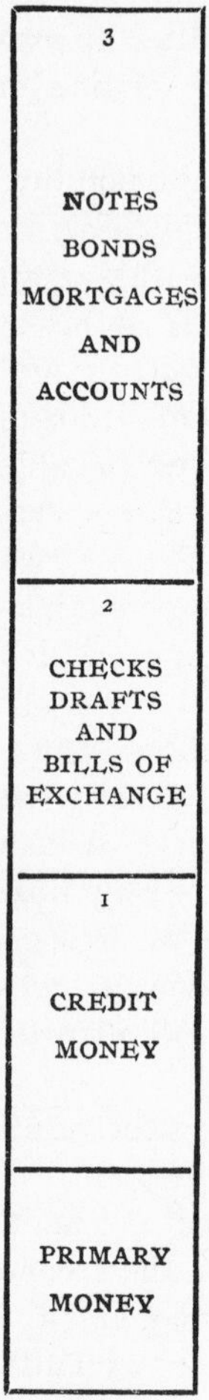

Fourth Lesson.

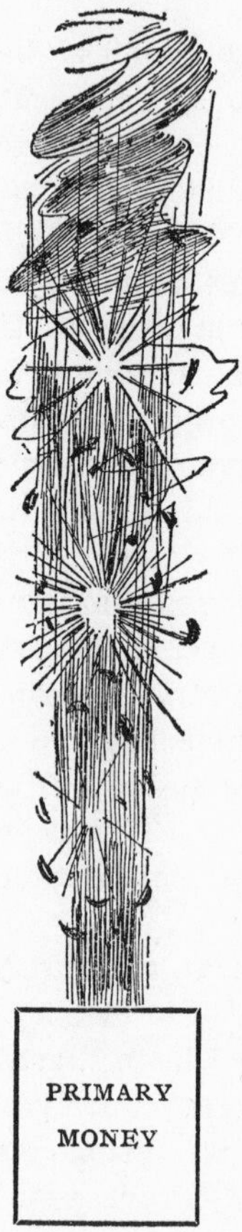

Fifth Lesson.

"Panics thus caused are of longer duration, and more disastrous than the first. They breed distrust in the money of the country; and with those who do not distinguish between primary money and credit money, the prejudice raised goes to the whole financial system. When demonetization took place, the column representing *primary money* was reduced a small percentage over one-half — for convenience we will say one-half—and this half that was demonetized was added to the first column of credits — credit money. The people, a short time *before* this was done, had been prosperous, and had expanded abnormally columns 2 and 3. So we then had conditions as illustrated in LESSON SIX.

"Though previously based on the declared intention to do so, actual resumption following the war, and a return to the system of property money, with credit money based thereon, did not take effect till January 1, 1879.

"For some time it was not generally known that silver was demonetized, and for many years since then its true position in our currency was disputed.

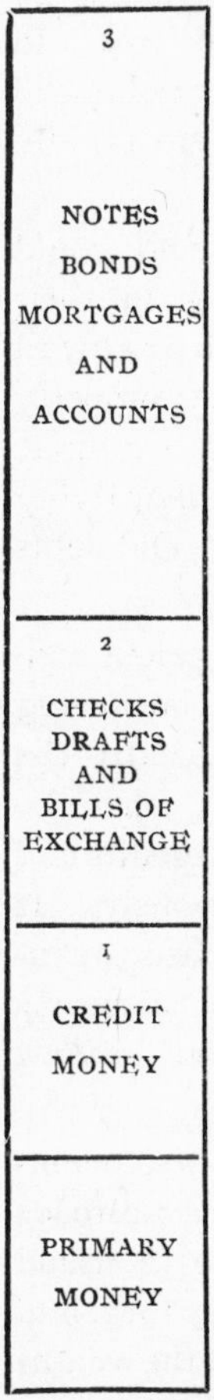

Sixth Lesson.

"It slowly dawned on the country that silver was neither fish nor fowl; that like Mahomed's coffin it swung half-way between the floor and ceiling.

"Finally the silver men, pushing their cause, forced the declaration from the administration that all paper money was redeemable in gold or silver at the option of the *holder*. This meant that they demanded the most favored and valuable of the two—gold. The government had stored most of the silver and issued paper money on it, which was declared to be redeemable in gold.

"This cut the base of the column half in two, and left us with only half a foundation for our financial system.

"This defined the position of silver as *token money*, and if not redeemed directly—gold for silver—the exchange of the silver for its paper representative would get the gold. The administration only wants a little more time to declare that silver is directly redeemable in gold—the true position of token money.

"In the meantime, during these years, all property gradually declined in value as

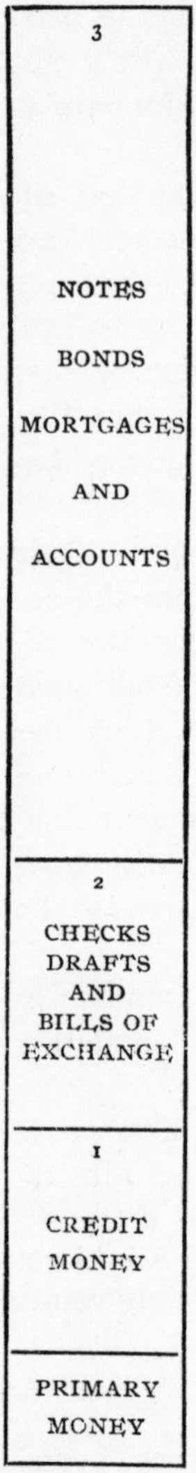

Seventh Lesson.

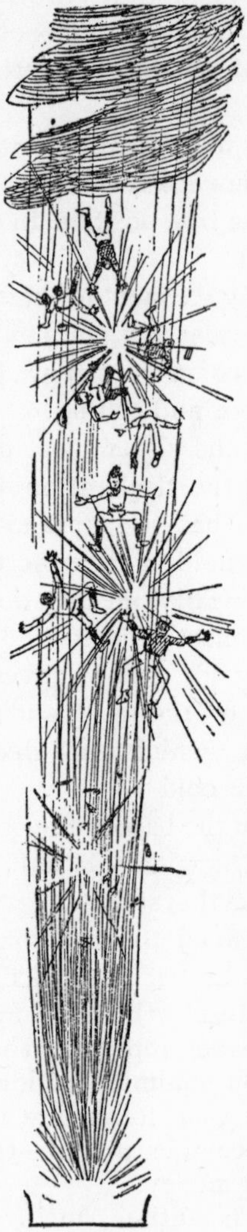

Eighth Lesson.

compared with gold. The decline was painfully steady.

"These conditions caused new debts to be contracted to pay old debts, and the volume of new debts were rapidly augmented.

"Those who could make nothing in their business borrowed money on their property to go into new ventures, and to meet their living expenses. Old debts were refunded.

"Falling prices continued, and borrowing continued until the spring of 1893, when the 3rd column of credits had grown enormously. It had now reached the incredible sum of nearly *forty thousand million dollars*.

"The bonded indebtedness of the railroads alone was five thousand million. Every town and city nearly felt the weight of a debt. Farms were mortgaged. Property in the cities was nearly all mortgaged.

"LESSON SEVEN shows the condition with us in 1890, just before the Baring failure.

"LESSON EIGHT shows the panic as it began in 1890—the result of the portentous financial conditions that had been brewing for a long time. A financial storm was now on the country, the rigor and duration of which was to be unprecedented in the history of the world. For it not only involved the first, second, and third columns of credit, but primary money itself was involved under the enormous strain placed upon it.

"By 1893 the conditions had grown worse, and LESSON NINE will illustrate it. (Applause.)

"The best barometer of the storm now are prices of products and labor; the first is still falling, and labor is not one-half employed. Judged by these the storm is growing worse.

"LESSON TEN will illustrate the present financial condition of the country. (Applause.)

"What is now needed is first to build up the redemption money of the country. By putting silver back in the column of redemption money we could increase it from its present volume of six hundred million to twelve hundred million. This amount of redemption money would warrant twelve hundred million of credit money.

"This would give us twenty-four hundred millions of money on a sound financial footing, or about $34 per capita. Whereas we now have virtually less than $20 per capita on an insufficient and unsound basis."

As COIN made this last statement he laid his right hand on the silver bell on the table, and as its clear notes rang through the room, a signal that the school

Ninth Lesson.

Tenth Lesson.

had adjourned for the day, a warm and hearty applause went up from a good percentage of the 2,500 people in the room.

A MEMBER OF THE FINANCIAL TRUST.

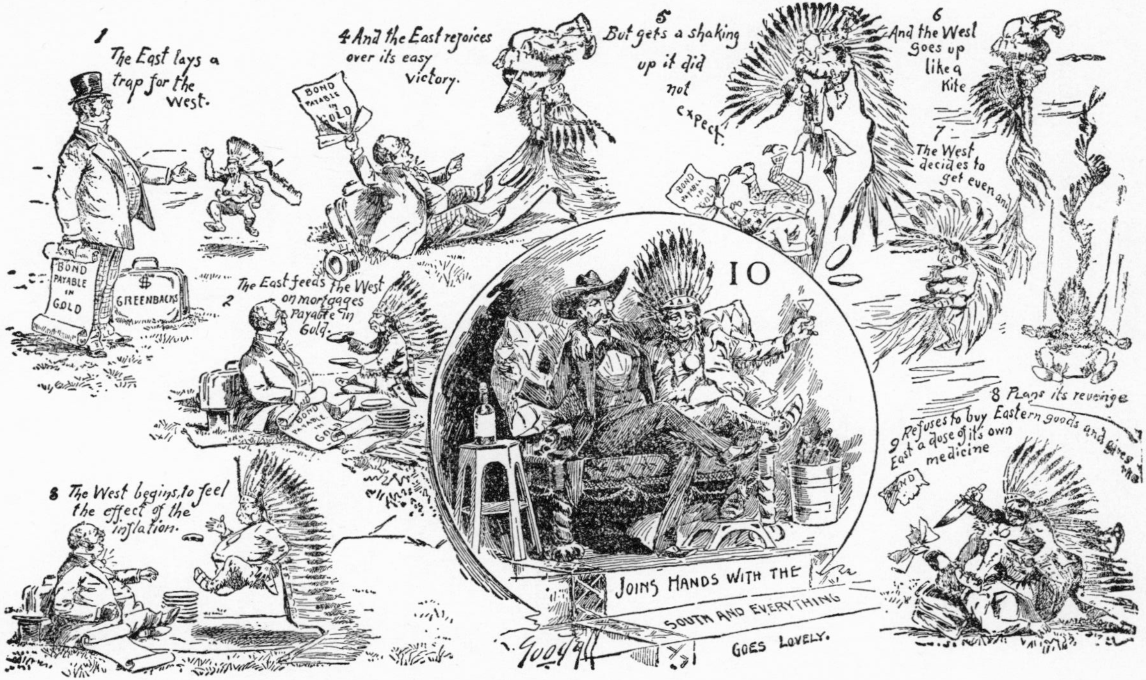
1 The East lays a trap for the West.
BOND PAYABLE IN GOLD
$ GREENBACKS
2 The East feeds the West on mortgages Payable in Gold.
BOND PAYABLE IN GOLD
4 And the East rejoices over its easy victory.
BOND PAYABLE IN GOLD
5 But gets a shaking up it did not expect.
BOND PAYABLE IN GOLD
6 And the West goes up like a Kite
7 The West decides to get even and
8 The West begins to feel the effect of the inflation.
8 Plans its revenge
9 Refuses to buy Eastern goods and gives East a dose of it's own medicine
BOND
10
JOINS HANDS WITH THE
SOUTH AND EVERYTHING
GOES LOVELY.
Goodall

THIRTY YEARS OF AMERICAN HISTORY—1870 TO 1900.

CHAPTER IV.

The Fourth Day.

The comments of the morning papers on the third day's session of the school on the whole were favorable. The published accounts had been full and substantially correct, and the *Times* and *Inter Ocean* reproduced the illustrations that had been used.

In this way the proceedings of the school had been laid before thousands of readers, whose interest had been aroused, and long before 10 o'clock the hall was crowded, and standing room could not be had.

The *Inter Ocean* in an editorial had commented on the tilt between Coin and Mr. Walsh, the president of the Chicago National Bank, and claimed that Coin had floored the great financier, in his answer to Mr. Walsh's proposition, that the government could not by legislation add to the commercial value of a commodity.

The *Times* pronounced the statements of Coin unanswerable; and said that interested parties had purposely kicked up a dust about silver, obscured and misrepresented the facts, and when confronted were unable to make good their statements, or answer the arguments of the bimetallists.

All who had been there on the previous days and who came early enough to get in were there, and many new faces could be seen in the audience.

Objection was raised by the audience to free admission. COIN was asked to admit people only on tickets, so seats could be procured, and to charge $2.00 a seat. This COIN agreed to with the understanding that the proceeds should go to the "soup houses" of Chicago, and this announcement was made just before the lecture for the day began, to take effect the next morning.

COIN had entered by a private door, and just at 10 o'clock came forward on the platform.

A DAY OF QUESTIONS.

He was met with a question at the beginning and it soon delevoped that it was to be a day of questions.

Professor Laughlin, head of the school of political economy in the Chicago University, an avowed monometallist, whose question had the attention of the whole house, said:

"You have stated since this school began, that so long as free coinage was enjoyed by both metals that the commercial value of silver and gold had never differed more than 2 per cent, and that this difference was accounted for by the disturbance of the French ratio and the cost of exchange. Am I right in so quoting you?"

"You are," replied COIN.

"Now, is it not a fact," said the professor, "that several times prior to 1857 silver coin sold at a premium as high as 8 per cent over gold?"

"Yes. That is true," replied COIN.

"Then why did you make the statement you did? And if what you now admit is true, then is there not liable at all times to be a wide margin between gold and silver which *free* coinage cannot control?"

"Professor," began COIN, with a smile on his handsome, young face. "I hardly think you are serious asking me that question. We were speaking of silver and gold bullion and not of silver coin. A demand often arises for small money. Suddenly change or small bills are found to be scarce in a large city. This was the case in New York last year, 1893, when silver dollars commanded a premium of 3 per cent—not because of the silver being worth more than a dollar—but because factories had to have small bills which they could not get to use in paying off their men. They paid the same premium for one and two dollar bills.

"A great inconvenience had arisen for the want of small money, and a premium had to be paid to get it. At the time you speak of, nearly all small money was made from silver, and on account of the French premium for silver our silver was leaving us. Small money was scarce, and frequently commanded a premium, not on account of the value of the silver bullion, but upon the demand for small money. Gold dollars commanded the same premium as silver dollars and fifty-cent pieces.

"If you are not satisfied with my answer I have the exchangeable quotations of silver and gold bullion at the time you speak of."

The professor had taken his seat. He now arose to say that he was satisfied with the answer.

"I am glad these questions are asked," said COIN. "These statements when used and not answered confuse the people."

THE LATIN UNION.

Mr. P. S. Eustis, General Passenger Agent of the C. B. & Q. Railroad, wanted to know what nations constituted the Latin Union, that COIN had referred to as having a ratio of 15½ to 1 prior to 1873.

"France, Belgium, Italy, Switzerland and Greece," was the reply.

"Then," said Mr. Eustis, "the Latin Union, Germany and the United States, by free coinage had maintained the commercial value of silver at par with gold?"

"Yes," was COIN'S reply.

"And the United States," said Mr. Eustis, "was the first of these to attack silver and demonetize it?"

"Yes," said COIN.

Mr. Eustis took his seat, and some one near him was heard to mutter, "It was old John Sherman."

SUPT. OF MAILS ASKS A QUESTION.

Mr. J. A. Montgomery, Superintendent of Mails at Chicago, then arose and asked this question:

"What would silver and gold be worth if neither were used as money?"

"That would depend," said the little financier, "on what was adopted as money to take their place and the quantity of it. Primary money becomes the measure of all values; and the value of any other commodity is more or less, as the quantity of primary money is more or less. That is the reason you hear gold referred to now as the standard or measure of values.

"The most impartial way to get at what the value of silver and gold would be if not used as money would be to suppose there was no money of any kind.

"Then there would be no measure of values, and only an exchange value would exist. If under these circumstances the arts and sciences progressed, the demand for silver and gold would cause other property to be exchanged for it, and as they are used in so many ways in the sciences and arts, and for domestic and ornamental purposes, it is reasonable to suppose they would have an exchange value equal to any other scarce property for which there was a demand.

"When it is considered that they are both precious

WILLIAM PENN BUYING PENNSYLVANIA.

metals—neither found in even or regular veins, and difficult and expensive to mine—it is not unreasonable to suppose that great store would be placed upon their possession when refined into the pure metal.

"Brass, copper, and other metals than silver and gold,

with anything like their specific gravity, discolor the skin when worn as ornaments.

"When we consider that the native Indians of this country were known to give up large quantities of valuable property *in exchange* for a few trinkets and ornaments, and that large domains of land were purchased in this way, it is natural to believe that a civilized man would give up as much as a bushel of wheat for the amount of silver in one of our silver fifty-cent pieces when fashioned into a ring.

"Cups, pitchers, spoons, table knives, and other forms of table ware made from or plated with silver or gold, will not stain either the liquids or food. Their use in manufacture, chemistry, and some other branches of the arts and sciences are now regarded as indispensable, and more than one-half of the total output of the world is so used.

"It has been said that silver and gold have no intrinsic value; this is not true. They are the only things used by Webster in the copy of his dictionary which I have to illustrate the meaning of the word 'intrinsic.'

"But exchange value, in the sense that a civilized or uncivilized person will barter or trade one property for another, is the primary value of all property.

"Iron cannot be used for food, but its utility gives it an exchange value. Silver can be utilized for many mechanical purposes for which iron serves, and can be adapted to a thousand uses where iron would not be suitable.

"Therefore, what the value of silver and gold would be if not used as money, to be expressed in dollars and cents, would depend, first, on what the new unit or dollar was, and then the abundance of the material from which it was being made; but when established, they would,

I think, have a value relatively with other property not much different from what they have had as the world's money."

COST OF PRODUCING SILVER.

Mr. M. L. Scudder, Jr., asked this question:

"Is it not a fact that silver can be mined for fifty cents an ounce, and does not the cost of production regulate its value?"

COIN replied as follows:

"It is not a fact that silver can be mined for fifty cents an ounce. In some particular mine, for a time, it may be mined for fifty cents an ounce, or less; just as gold has been mined for a time in Australia and California for ten per cent of its value."

"You must not judge of the cost of mining precious metals by any one mine; or by mining coal, iron, or other metals and minerals that lay in even veins. The latter class is demonstrated by geological formation and experience to be reliable in quality and quantity; works are erected, and conservative management and business judgment are safely applied to its production.

"Not so with silver and gold mines. They are most unreliable in both quality and quantity. Costly buildings and machinery are often erected to economize the mining of the ore, only to find no mine to operate by the time the buildings are completed and the machinery is working.

"Silver and gold are found in uneven and broken veins and pockets. Sometimes the 'pay streak' is a foot wide, to narrow down to an inch a few feet farther on. A single blast has been known to 'blow out' a mine —and with it the hopes of those who before the shot was fired thought they were millionaires.

"A silver mine that will assay 100 ounces to the ton at 200 feet depth, has been known to run only 10 ounces at 400 feet depth. The Yankee Girl mine in Red Mountain, Colorado, was a heavy dividend payer, at 300 feet, and the ore was too low grade to pay to hoist at 800 feet. The Comstock mines changed at 1,600 feet from high grade to low grade ore. The reverse is just as often true. Mines that are low grade near the surface are high grade with depth.

"It is estimated by all men of judgment who have given practical attention to mining, that the silver now in existence has cost not less than $2.00 per ounce, and many put it much higher.

"Mining for silver and gold has a speculative and gambling feature to it, that will lure men on notwithstanding the great cost, because a few 'strike it rich'; just as men will speculate on the Board of Trade, though in the end ten lose to where one gains. If Mr. Scudder's proposition were true, you would all be engaged in silver mining.

SAM B. RAYMOND.

"But your presence here gives me an opportunity to forever set this question at rest. I am sure that in so large an assemblage of wealthy Chicago men, many of you have had some experience in silver mining. Now, if all of you," and COIN began to smile, "who have lost money in mining for silver will rise to your feet, I will then call on those who have made by it to stand up also."

The applause indicated clearly that the young economist had clinched his point; and the smile that went round told that the shot had gone home.

Sitting in the assembly were many prominent Chi-

WHAT IT COST SOME MEN

cago citizens who had invested in silver mining and had made a sufficient test to satisfy themselves both as to the risk incurred and the cost per ounce of mining silver.

A GREENBACKER.

Mr. E. R. Ridgeley, of Ogden, Utah, who was in the audience, said he would like to ask a question.

"Proceed," said COIN.

"I want to know," said Mr. Ridgeley, 'if it is not practical to maintain a purely greenback system."

"Yes," said COIN. "The only theory, however, on which a purely greenback or paper money system might be maintained would be to do away with a redemption money entirely. You cannot have both without the redemption principle applying. The money with a value in itself becomes the most preferable, and must stand behind the other.

WILLIAM T. BAKER.

"You cannot maintain two kinds of money at a parity, when one has a commercial value and the other has none, except by making one redeemable in the other.

"But you might have a purely paper money. The method would be to have no redemption money and to make it legal tender in the payment of all debts public and private.

"Limit it in quantity by fixing the amount at so much *per capita*. Maintain the volume at that as population increased, and from time to time provide for what had been destroyed. The fact that it was limited in quantity, and the uses for which it was intended, would give it a value, and make it a measure of values, and a serviceable medium of exchange.

PRESENT TO PRODUCE SILVER.

"Silver and gold would be treated as any other merchandise, and would be purchased at their market value, and exported to other countries, where they might be used as money, or for use in this or other countries in the arts and sciences."

GEORGE H. WHEELER.

"Then," said Mr. Ridgeley, "what objection is there to such a system?"

"The objection which is urged," said COIN, "is this: So long as there was confidence in the government, it would be a sound, stable money. But so soon as confidence in the government was shaken it would depreciate in exchangeable value.

When the danger became imminent that the government was not able to enforce its legal tender character, having no commercial value, it would become more or less worthless.

"The paper or substance out of which it is made, would have no exchangeable value, unlike money made from a valuable commodity; when much disturbed by a lack of confidence it would fluctuate in value; and if the government went down it would be entirely worthless.

MARTIN J. RUSSELL.

"Money with a commercial value makes a medium of exchange with the balance of the world, and facilitates our trade."

"But," said Mr. Ridgeley, who was still standing: "Isn't it a fact, that when war, and great disturbances come, that redemption money disappears, and paper money takes its place anyhow? So are not the

WHAT IT COST SOME MEN

people at such times embarrassed with a paper money fluctuating with their confidence in the government, and saddled with a worthless paper money if the government goes down, and does the use of silver and gold as money ever prevent this condition from arising?'

GEN'L JOHN C. BLACK.

"The use of redemption money," replied Coin, "does not prevent the conditions you describe. Paper money always takes its place at such times. The people, however, are not injured by it. They store away their good money—and have it in their possession ready to use at any time, and it becomes especially useful if the other money should become entirely worthless.

"After the use of redemption money ceases because of war, every one is on the same footing. As the paper money fluctuates from day to day, all are taking chances alike. If it becomes wholly worthless, all have suffered more or less proportionately, and primary money immediately takes its place.

ROSEWELL MILLER.

"This latter is true, whether a new government is founded on the ruins of the old one at once or not. There may be a long interregnum, as in France toward the close of the last century, when one form of government was from year to year almost, substituted for another. No one knew what was coming next. No stability was in the government itself. During such a period, which may last for years, it would be impossible to make paper money circulate. But money made from property having a commercial value would circulate, and would assist materially in restoring order and civilization. In fact, it would be hard to restore civilization without its use during such a period.

CHARLES NAGL.

"We are approaching such a period now, unless wise statesmanship shall intervene; commodity money—silver and gold—will be our only money, and will have to answer the purpose of a medium of exchange until a stable government can get on its feet and issue *paper* money.

"All know and feel the necessity of money, and if chaos comes in this country, it may be years before there is another government sufficiently established to give confidence generally to its issue of paper money.

"In the meantime silver and gold coin will be the only thing on which we can rely for money, and of the two silver will be as it always has been, the greatest friend of the people."

MONEY BASED ON LABOR.

J. R. Sovereign, Master Workman of the Knights of Labor, who had a seat on the platform, now asked a question:

J. FOSTER RHODES.

"You have given us the theory and science of money," said Mr. Sovereign, "as based on *property*. I want to know if it is practical to issue a form of credit money based on *labor?*"

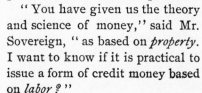

WHAT IT COST SOME MEN

"Yes," said Coin. "It is practical, and, to the extent to which it could be brought into use, would be on a parity with other forms of money based on property.

"Suppose the government owned and controlled all the railroads—it could issue paper money redeemable in services. That is, it would be good in the payment of freight and at all the ticket offices.

JOHN S. COOPER.

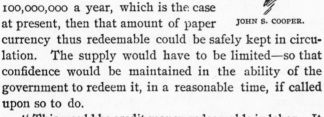

"If the passenger and freight business of the country amounted to $1,100,000,000 a year, which is the case at present, then that amount of paper currency thus redeemable could be safely kept in circulation. The supply would have to be limited—so that confidence would be maintained in the ability of the government to redeem it, in a reasonable time, if called upon so to do.

"This would be credit money redeemable in labor. It should also be made legal tender, and differ in no respect from credit money redeemable in property—silver and gold—except as to the nature of redemption.

WILLIAM LINDSAY.

"Naturally it would circulate side by side with the other form of credit money, inside of the United States, and in the payment of freight and purchase of transportation, no discrimination would ordinarily be made in the form of money used.

"If confidence in the existence of the government should be shaken by wars or disintegration, as such a danger arose, this form of money would be assorted out

PRESENT TO PRODUCE SILVER.

from the other and redemption could take place, and no one would suffer by it.

J. M. ROACH.

"It would be as sound a currency as credit money based on property.

"It would be put in circulation by the government paying it out to its employés.

"The postage stamp is based on the principle of redemption in services, but is not issued in suitable form for currency, and yet it is frequently used in small remittances in letters as such.

"A form of credit money could now be issued resembling our paper bills, redeemable in postage stamps."

"How much?" asked Mr. Sovereign, whose face had worn a broad smile during the answer to his previous question.

"The total annual postal business," said COIN, "of the government for last year was about $75,000,000. This amount would circulate at par, with other money—how much more I would not now undertake to say. It would be redeemable in postage stamps, just as the other would be redeemable in railroad passenger tickets, or receipted freight bills.

POTTER PALMER.

"This would be money based on labor."

NO SPECIAL ADVANTAGE TO SILVER STATES.

COIN was here interrupted by President Struckman, of the Board of County Commissioners, who said:

"Is it not unfair to give the owners of silver bullion the special privilege of having the value of their property enhanced? Is it not virtually making a present of millions of dollars to the owners of silver bullion by remonetizing silver? Is this just or right?"

"In the first place," replied COIN, "whatever you select as primary money should be treated distinctively different from all other property. It should not be left on the market to be bulled or beared. Otherwise you cannot have a stable money.

"Free coinage at a fixed quantity to constitute a dollar does take it off the market, and that is what is necessary in the treatment of a money metal. That is the way gold is now treated, and silver should be so treated.

"But your statement is not true. Silver men are not benefited by remonetization except in common with others. Silver is now worth about 60 cents an ounce as measured in the new standard—gold. It was worth $1.29 per ounce under free coinage. The owner of silver bullion can now buy as much with an ounce of silver as he ever could.

PRESIDENT STRUCKMAN ASKS A QUESTION.

An ounce of silver bullion, worth $1.29 in 1873, would *in 1873* buy a bushel of wheat; and an ounce of silver bullion worth 60 cents now, as measured in gold, *will buy a bushel of wheat now.* It took three ounces of silver bullion to buy a keg of nails in 1873, and two ounces will buy a keg of nails now. An ounce of silver bullion ($1.29) would buy 16 yards of calico in 1873, and it (60 cents) will buy 16 yards of calico now.

"The exchange value of uncoined silver with the other products is substantially the same now as it ever was. Where silver producers are hurt is only in common with all producers—stagnation, falling prices, paralysis of business, and confiscation of property by taxation and debts that *do not shrink* with all other values."

COIN'S answer was satisfactory. This was evident not from applause, for there was none; but from the intense stillness and breathless attention. It was also attested from the further fact that there sat in the audience men ready to leap upon him at the least show. His answers had to be absolutely convincing, or an antagonist was there ready to puncture the weak places. Not one opened his mouth. COIN was like a little monitor in the midst of a fleet of wooden ships. His shots went through and silenced all opposition.

PROFESSORS OF POLITICAL ECONOMY.

There was Professor Laughlin still irritated at his unsuccessful attack on the little bimetallist. As the professor in a chair of political economy, endowed with the money of bankers, his mental faculties had trained with his salary, but his views had been those of theory. Those views now encountered the practical statesman. He moved nervously in his chair, but said nothing.

Here was a study and an object-lesson. Combined capital all over the world had been using professors of political economy to instruct the minds of young men to a belief in the gold standard. This is not hard to do, as these students, being young, their minds are easily molded. The error is planted deep and strong.

Anything can be proved by theoretical reasoning. In the practical application of a theory is the proof of its strength. The gold standard, now fitted to a shivering world, is squeezing the life out of it. The men of the country, the backbone of the republic, on whose strong arms the life of the nation may depend, are delivering over their property to their creditors, and going into beggary. This is the test proof of the beneficence of monometallism.

There sat a representative professor on political economy, at home when with his school boys, but powerless and confused in the presence of an adversary who courted his questions, but which he knew it was useless to propound.

"You do not enrich the people of the silver states one cent by the remonetization of silver," continued COIN, "except in common with the people of the state of Illinois, and of the whole United States.

"You increase the value of all property by adding to the number of money units in the land. You make it possible for the debtor to pay his debts ; business to start anew, and revivify all the industries of the country, which must remain paralyzed so long as silver as well as all other property is measured by a gold standard.

Mr. Struckman interrupted COIN to say, that the answer to his proposition was entirely satisfactory. That the reply given had never occurred to him, simple as it was. That he wanted to say further, he considered that the people of Chicago had been imposed on by some of their great newspapers ; what private object they had, or whose interests they were serving, he did not know ; but they had misrepresented the silver question. He felt better to make this open confession, and he thought other gold-bugs would feel better if they would do likewise.

IMPROVED FACILITIES.

Mr. Kirk, President of the American Exchange National Bank, was now seen standing up, and COIN stopped to hear the question he was about to put.

"Have not the improved facilities for production," asked Mr. Kirk, "caused a general lowering of prices, and is not this mainly responsible for the gradual decline since 1873?"

COIN replied:

"Improved facilities for production have not been continuous when applied to any one article in the sense of explaining the decline in prices.

"Nearly everything except gold has declined largely in the last two years—the average is about twenty-five per cent—and it may be said that little or no improved facilities have come into use during that time. Demonetization and the collapse of our financial system seems to have paralyzed the hand of even the inventor, and yet values continue to decline.

"Improved facilities as a rule do have a tendency to lower prices, but it is only an incident, and not the cause of the overthrow of our industries.

"When the demand is greater than the supply, prices may advance at the very time that improved facilities for production are in progress.

"Improved facilities for mining gold, both in the placer and quartz mines, are continuously being applied; and yet the value of that metal, in purchasing power, is continuously rising.

"Take the case of wool. There has been no improved facilities for making it grow on the backs of sheep, or of shearing them, in the last twenty years, and yet wool is only about one-third the price it was a few years ago. It, with many other articles that can be put in the same class, have been steadily declining in price as expressed in terms of dollars and cents.

"A gentleman from Oregon, now in the audience, tells me that he has lately seen horses in his state sell at auction for 75 cents each. And that horses in droves have been offered there recently at one cent a pound at private sale, with no one willing to take them. It can not be said, that there are any improved facilities, for raising horses."

THE TARIFF PROPOSITION.

Mr. H. H. Kohlsaat, late proprietor of the *Inter Ocean*, now said that he wanted to say something, and as he had COIN'S attention, immediately proceeded to state the tariff proposition. Mr. Kohlsaat claimed that the threat to reduce or abolish tariff, in his opinion, had more to do with the hard times than anything else. That since attending these lectures he had more than ever recognized the damage demonetization had done; but he still thought the tariff an important question.

In replying COIN admitted that a large business interest was more or less disturbed when it was proposed to change the tariff schedule. With manufacturers it was not so much a question of how much the tariff is, as what it is, and so long as that was in doubt it was a disturbing element.

"But," said COIN, "we are trying to get at what is the main or underlying cause of our present industrial demoralization, and tariff, pro or con, will not account for it. Our decline in values has been going on steadily and persistently since the demonetization of silver. During that period we have had different tariff bills, and of late years a very high tariff schedule, and yet it has had no effect in stopping the fall of prices.

"What more clearly than anything else demonstrates that tariff is not the trouble we are searching out, is that the same business depression existing in the United States also prevails in Europe, Australia, and all countries where gold has been made the standard and measure of values.

"To see only our own trouble, and attribute it to local causes, is to be like the narrow-minded Chicago man who attributes the present depression, to the World's Fair.

"The Chicago *Post* published the following the other day from the San Francisco *Chronicle*, that will forcibly illustrate my answer to this question;" and COIN read the following:

The San Francisco *Chronicle*, says advices from Australia by the steamer Warrimoo show an alarming increase in casualties, crimes and acute distress. The police are unable to cope with

BANK PANIC OF 1893.

ALL GOLD STANDARD COUNTRIES AFFECTED.

desperate housebreakers, who swarm in the large cities. A few that have been arrested give as an excuse that famine drove them to deeds of violence. Several of the policemen attacked by burglars at Sydney are dying. The survivors have been promoted and given bonuses by Sir George Gibbs.

On one day last week at Sydney, besides a score of petty robberies, the City Hospital was robbed of all its valuables by nurses;

Mercredie & Drew, manufacturers, were robbed of fifty thousand dollars by employés; F. Coxon, merchant, was robbed by an employé of a large sum. Three young women succeeded in passing a number of counterfeit checks. Charles Graham, a post-office clerk, embezzled two hundred dollars from the postoffice.

The government's claim is that the unemployed problem is too complicated to solve. In Sydney five hundred dollars each week is spent in aiding five hundred families. Five thousand men in South Australia asked the Governor to call a special session of Parliament to discuss means to aid them. The Governor refused. Then they waited on Premier Kingston, but the Premier would promise nothing. He told them that though they were in want of food, they had refused to break a yard and a half of rock per week for rations, and he could do no more. The delegation said that they would not break rock for food alone.

Thousands are sleeping in the open air and several have starved to death. At Bourke Afghans and Europeans quarreled over a division of labor, and a bloody row occurred. The most tragic suicides out of ninety-eight in one week, directly the result of hard times, are: F. W. Wilson, the biscuit manufacturer of Brisbane, shot himself; William O'Connor, lodger in the European Hotel, Melbourne, jumped from the fourth story and dashed his brains out on the pavement; Kate Brooks, a pretty English girl, starving, got drunk and killed herself with poison; Joseph Bancroft, a miner, out of work, said good-bye to his family and exploded a cartridge in his mouth.

As COIN closed the reading of the extract from the *San Francisco Chronicle*, Mr. Joel Bigelow asked him to read an extract from a paper published in London called "*The Colonies and India*" which Mr. Bigelow then had in his hand. COIN consenting, Mr. Bigelow came forward with the paper, and COIN read the extract as follows:

One of our contemporaries asks: "What is the most constant standard of value in existence?" There can be but one rational answer, in fact—viz., silver. The value of a ton weight of silver on any given day—whether expressed in *£. s. d.*, in dollars and cents, in francs, in marks, or in rupees and pice, and (compared on the same day with) the sum of the market prices of standard test quantities of each of one hundred varieties of the most generally-dealt-in commodities of the market, also expressed in the same money terms—have by statistical observation and many hundreds of official tests, practically been found the constant equivalent, on the same market, of each other during the last five and twenty years since the system of "index numbers" was invented and applied to this branch of national business. This fact stands officially recorded. For Great Britain the Board of Trade publishes tables which prove it, and such, or their own private statistics, are regularly printed in leading commercial journals. Continental scientists also regularly publish their independent statements of these "index numbers." The truly marvelous fact above stated is thus capable of absolute verification by each one for himself, and if this does not prove silver to be the true and world-wide standard of value then there is no significance in facts. The metal gold, on the contrary, tried by the same supreme test, shows itself to be in no sense a "standard" of value, for it jumps about like the mercury in a barometer with every movement of the commercial atmosphere, its vibrations—to speak within the fact—having dodged about, up and down, as much as 20 per cent. down from a given point and then back to that point, and then 20 per cent. up from that same point, all within the short space of 40 or 50 years! How in the name of commercial sanity, how with a profession of national honesty, how with a claim to the meanest common sense, the Government of England continues to oppose the restoration of our ancient, proved, and only honest standard of value passes the wit of sane onlookers to understand.

MAYOR HOPKINS ASKS A QUESTION.

Mayor Hopkins wanted to know what effect the adoption of the gold standard by the governments using it had, if any, on those nations using a silver or bimetallic standard. What effect, if any, it had on their prosperity?

COIN'S reply was: "If a bimetallic or silver standard nation, or its people, are largely in debt, with the obligations payable in gold, the effect is serious. Take our South American republics to illustrate it: During the last 30 years they have been getting deeper and deeper into debt to England, and during the last 25 years these debts have been made payable in gold.

"Each year, with the advance in gold it takes more and more of their products, or silver, to pay the gold bonds; they must give up in silver $1.25 to pay $1 in gold—$1.50 in silver to pay $1 in gold—$1.75 in silver to pay $1 in gold, and so on, as the purchasing power of gold advances; and at the present time $2 in silver to pay $1 in gold.

So that a bond for $100,000 executed by them when silver and gold were at a parity, payable in gold, must now be met by the payment in principal of $200,000 in their money. That is—to raise the $100,000 in gold, they must sell 200,000 of their silver dollars. You will notice in the London Financial reports the price of Mexican dollars as 50 cents or 49 cents as the case may be; which means that about two Mexican silver dollars are accepted in payment for one dollar in gold settlements.

"The bonds of these countries both national and private are held in England for large amounts, and the enhanced value of gold is having a very serious effect on their prosperity. We are now an ally of England in depressing the price of silver and enhancing the value of gold.

"*We* are paying England 200 million dollars annually in gold in the payment of interest on our bonds, national and private, owned by her people, and to meet this annual interest *we* are giving up about 400 million dollars in property that is required in the market to secure the 200 million in gold.

"Our silver dollars are at par with gold by reason

only of our enforcement of the gold standard—redeeming silver with gold. Otherwise we are with reference to debts in the same fix as our Southern neighbors, with this difference; while they settle their foreign debts only in gold, we settle *both foreign and domestic debts on the gold basis*, and in each instance part with about two portion of property in settlement for one portion of debt."

And with this COIN announced the close of the lecture for the day.

As he did so Mr. Stone, secretary of the Chicago Board of Trade, stood up in his chair in the center of the hall, and addressing COIN, said:

"The members of the Board of Trade would like to attend to-morrow's lecture, but the regular session of the board lasts till 1 p. m.; if it could be arranged to have the 'school' open at 2 p. m. instead of 10 a. m., it would make it possible for us to be present. And in that event I am commissioned to buy three hundred tickets for to-morrow's lecture. We feel a special interest in what shall take place here to-morrow, as I am creditably informed the price of wheat will be discussed."

COIN consented to the request made by Mr. Stone, and the time for opening the school on the next day, Friday, was set for 2 p. m.

Mr. H. M. Milliken, a young bimetallist was selected by COIN as manager and treasurer of the hall under the new system adopted of charging for seats. Mr. Stone at once selected and paid for three hundred seats, to be occupied by members of the Board of Trade.

COTTON
7 cents
WEST
NEW YORK

CHAPTER V.

THE FIFTH DAY.

It was a day of bulls and bears.

Tickets for seats had been printed the evening previous, and the ticket office had been opened in the morning.

Under Mr. Milliken's able management, notwithstanding the great rush, everything proceeded orderly; and after the seats were all sold, tickets for standing room readily brought the regular price, until the hall was packed. There were fully 3,000 people in the audience at two o'clock, when COIN appeared on the crowded platform.

The morning papers had twitted Professor Laughlin with his attempt to trap the little bimetallist by an unfair question, and the *Times* cited it as a sample of the methods used by the monometallists in their campaign of misrepresentations.

Lengthy comments were published editorially on the proposition of credit money based on labor, to be redeemed in services by the government.

The *Inter Ocean* said, editorially:

> This kind of money would relieve the volume of money now used in transactions with the numerous postoffices of the whole United States. It is no inconsiderable amount that is now required to perform this business, and the country would readily absorb a supply sufficient for a year's use in advance.

The *Record* said:

The idea of money based on labor is a new one, but the plan is so practical and sensible, we can see no objection to it. To enlarge its use necessitates the government ownership of railroads. Government ownership of the telegraph lines would also add to the quantity of this class of money. It would certainly be sound money, redeemable in value received in the way of services.

There would be no serious objection to government ownership of railroads and telegraph lines if all of the employés were disfranchised. If they had no power to vote there would be no danger of *Cæsarism* from them. If the country was prosperous, and all branches of business were lucrative, the number of people desiring to hold a government situation would be materially reduced.

COIN'S answer to Mr. Scudder, as to the cost of producing silver, was approved by all the papers except the *Tribune*. But as that paper has become the unblushing defender of the classes, on the income tax, bribed and unjust property assessments, and every other iniquity that bears heavily on the many and favors a few, little importance was attached to what it said.

The monometallists that were such from personal interest had been piqued and disappointed at the headway the little bimetallist was making. His lectures were having an influence that speeches, books and articles could not have, as he was challenging contradiction of his statements. With such an audience of students of finance, authors and bankers, these statements became admitted facts, that in their judgment were dangerous to their cause.

Two columns had been erected on the platform for this morning, and each of these were surmounted by a sheaf of wheat. This was due to the good taste of Mr. Milliken, by whose direction it had been arranged.

Three globes were on the platform. One was very large and the other two were very small.

The little economist began his fifth lecture with a compliment to the Chicago Board of Trade, as the greatest institution of its character in the world. He then proceeded as follows:

"The total value of all the property in the world is about 450,000 million dollars.

"The available silver and gold money of the world combined is about 7,500 million dollars. The available gold money in the world is about 3,750 million dollars.

"Their proportion in values to each other is represented by these three globes." COIN pointed, as he said this, to the three globes on the platform by him, and then picked up the two smaller ones and held them in his hand that the audience might see them. He then continued:

"The large one represents the value of all the real and personal property in the world; the larger of the two small ones represents the face value of the silver and gold in the world available for use as money; and the smallest represents the amount of gold in the world available for use as money. The proportion of these globes to each other is in the same ratio as the figures I have named.

"The large one is 60 times as large as this one," indicating the second in size, "representing silver and gold, and is 120 times as large as the small one which represents gold. In estimating this wealth of the world, property in some countries has been measured in a silver standard, in others in a gold standard, and in others in a standard gradually shifting from a bimetallic to a gold standard. All are based on figures of 1890.

QUANTITATIVE THEORY OF MONEY.

"The value of the property of the world, as expressed in money, depends on what money is made of, and how much money there is.

"All writers on political economy admit the quantitative theory of money. Common sense confirms it.

"To be correct this theory should always be applied to the quantity of redemption money.

"The issuing of wheat certificates against the wheat in your elevators, does not increase the value of the wheat; and the credit money issued against the redemption money, does not increase the value of property. It facilitates business based thereon. It enlarges business—not values.

"The exchange value of primary money, for the property of the world, and *vice versa*, fixes the comparative value of the two.

"So if the quantity of *money* is large, the total value of the property of the world will be correspondingly large as expressed in dollars or money units. If the quantity of *money* is small, the total value of the property of the world will be correspondingly reduced.

"Property measures its value in money, and money measures its value in property. Money may increase in value by reason of its scarcity. When this is the case it buys more property—property buys less money.

"The same law of supply and demand applies to it as applies to any specific class of property. You are of all men most familiar with that law of trade.

"If a certain number of bushels of wheat, is a normal supply for the world's use, and only half that quantity of wheat is produced, what is the result? Wheat is worth about twice as much per bushel as if the normal amount had been raised. A bushel of wheat will buy twice as much money as it would have bought if there had been a normal quantity.

"This rule applies to money. If there is a normal quantity, it measures its value in property at a certain price, subject to supply and demand affecting property only. If a normal quantity of money on a sound financial basis is maintained, values of property, and debts with reference to the time of contraction and payment, will be equitably adjusted, and fluctuations in values will depend

GOLD UP, AND COMMODITIES DOWN.

on locality, and supply and demand of property, not money.

"At present the redemption money of the world in some countries is silver, and in some gold. Until recently the two were combined as primary money in most of the world under a law of free coinage, as we have before considered. Now silver is being destroyed as primary money, by a general movement that is deranging the commerce of the world, and the stronger nations are compelling the silver-using nations to settle with them on the gold basis.

"It is therefore proposed by the monometallists to measure the value of all property in gold, and to settle all debts in gold or in money redeemable in gold. If our debts were payable in wheat, wheat certificates which you handle every day would answer the same purpose, but the wheat would have to be in existence. So it is, if our debts are payable in gold—if paid in other money *it* must be as good as gold. To be as good as gold the other money must be redeemable in gold, just as your wheat certficates, are redeemable in wheat.

QUANTITY OF GOLD IN THE WORLD.

"This policy rests upon the quantity of gold in the world.

"To carry out such a financial policy the world has, as reported by the director of the U. S. Mint, about 3,750 million of dollars in gold. Under any calculation it will not exceed at the present time 3,900 million dollars.

"But let us take the larger figure, 3,900 million dollars, and see what this amount means.

"The population of the world in 1890 was about 1,400 million. It is a *per capita* for the population of the world of about $2.50. In bulk it is about one-half the size of this nickel I hold in my hand." And as COIN said this he held up a 5-cent piece between his thumb and forefinger.

"The whole 3,900 million dollars of gold in the world, cast into cubic foot blocks, can be stacked up in the corner of this room in a space 22 feet square and 22 feet high, and space enough will be left of the 22 feet each way to box it in."

COIN here directed two boys, with a stick and tape line in their hands, to go to the corner of the room and measure off 22 feet square.

This they did, with the assistance of the people sitting there; measuring from the corner 22 feet each way along the walls, and then out from those points 22 feet parallel with the first measurements. At this point the stick that one of the boys was carrying was placed in a perpendicular position, with the tape line reaching each way 22 feet to the walls.

COIN, continuing, said:

"That stick is 22 feet high, and the inclosure indicated by it and the tape line is the cube of 22 feet. *That space will hold all the gold in the world obtainable for use as money!*"

COIN had spoken the last few words slowly but with great emphasis. A buzz of conversation went around the room with expressions of disbelief—such as "impossible," "it cannot be." Many had risen to their feet. Professor Laughlin was scratching his head. A mild state of sensation pervaded the entire room. The bimetallists were excited, but smiling, for they felt confident the little financier could not be cornered. In fact, he now had gold in the corner.

"A cubic foot of cast gold," continued COIN, after waiting for the effect of his last words, "weighs 19,258 ounces; multiply this by 480, the number of grains in an ounce, and you have 9,243,840 grains.

"This gives you the number of grains in a cubic foot of gold. There are 23.22 (to be exact) grains of gold in a dollar; divide the number of grains in a cubic foot by this, and it gives you the number of dollars, viz.: $398,098 in a cubic foot of cast gold.

"Now as there is $398,098 in a cubic foot of gold, by

dividing this sum into $3,900,000,000, the outside estimate on the total gold supply of the world, we get as a result 9,796 cubic feet. The next question is, how much space will 9,796 cubic feet occupy. Instead of extracting the cube root, which would be unintelligible to many, we will do it this way."

And with this he turned to the blackboard and multiplied 22 by 22, and that result by 22 again—thus giving the number of cubic feet in a space 22 feet each way. The result was 10,648.

"You see," said COIN, "a space 22 feet each way, such as I have marked off in the corner of the room, contains 10,648 cubic feet.

The total number of cubic feet of gold in the world is 9,796. So we could put it all in that inclosure, and have 852 cubic feet of space left, which you will admit is enough to box it all in, without requiring any more of the space of this valuable room than the 22 feet.*

"This block of gold could be put in the wheat pit of the Chicago Board of Trade," continued COIN, looking down at the members of the Board of Trade who had front seats, "and you could go on buying and selling wheat without its seriously interfering with your business."

With this COIN paused, and another buzz of conversation went around the room. Excited astonishment was upon the faces of all. There stood the figures, and no one could longer disbelieve.

MEASURING THE GOLD.

"I will show you," he continued "how you can test this statement in a simple way. It is best that not

*A cubic foot of water weighs 1,000 ounces. The specific gravity of cast gold is 19.258. Of silver 10.474. To get the weight of a cubic foot of gold or silver multiply 1,000 by these figures respectively.

the least scintilla of doubt should remain in your minds as to the truth of any statement that I make. The people have been too long deceived by misrepresentations; the world has been brought to its present condition of misery by deception on this subject and we must depend on truth to find permanent lodgement in your minds to root out the falsehood.

ALL THE GOLD OF THE WORLD IN THE CHICAGO WHEAT PIT

"I have here the teller of the Metropolitan National Bank with 125 twenty-dollar gold pieces, the number necessary for this simple test."

As COIN said this the teller of the Metropolitan National Bank stepped forward with a sachel in his hand. COIN then laid a foot-rule down on the table and placed 9 twenty-dollar gold pieces by it. Those on the platform gathered around, while he explained to the audience that nine twenty-dollar gold pieces placed in a row was one foot long, and that hence eighty-one of them would go in a square foot.

He then stacked up the gold pieces a foot high, placing the rule by the side of them, and announced that the 125 in the stack measured one foot.

And then said :

"Multiply 81, the number in a square foot, by 125, the number in each stack, to make them all a foot high, and you have as a result 10,125 twenty-dollar gold pieces. Multiply this by twenty, the value of each, and you get the value of this cubic foot of gold coins, viz., $202,500.

"A cubic foot of gold coin has in it 10 per cent of alloy ; this, together with the unoccupied space between the stacks of coin, is nearly as much space as that occupied by the pure gold in the coins. So you can see that if it was pure solid cast gold the cubic foot would contain the $398,098+.

"All the gold in the world cast into solid blocks may be stacked behind the counter of the Metropolitan National Bank."

Coin then turned to the teller and invited him to a seat on the platform until he reached the silver illustration.

"Most of your offices would hold it all," Coin began again.

"It is in this quantity of gold that it is proposed to measure the value of all the other property of the world. Its significance is written in our present low prices and depression in business.

"When the transformation now going on in India, which is changing her from the silver standard to a gold standard, and when Mexico and South America, and the balance of the world are added to the gold standard, should such be the case, one pinch from that block of gold the size of a gold dollar (one-twentieth of an ounce) will be so valuable that it will not only buy two bushels of wheat, as it does now, but it will then buy four bushels of wheat.

"One-half that quantity will buy ten hours' labor from a strong-armed mechanic. So much as you could put in the palm of your hand, will then buy a man's soul —a statesman's honor. It is breaking down the fabric of our institutions; driving hope from the heart and happiness from the minds of our people." And with a voice low and impassioned that reached the finer fibres of every heart in that room, he added: "Who can estimate the damage to the commerce and business of the world? Who can estimate the suffering that humanity has and must yet experience? In what language can we characterize the men behind the scenes who knowingly are directing this world to the gold standard?"

A man rising in the middle of the audience, exclaimed, with the accent of Ireland in his tones: "Imps of hell unchained, banqueting in selfish glee upon the heart's blood of the world." It came with the Irish ring in the words, rich and mellow, yet breathing fire and vengeance —vengeance for wrongs seared into the human heart suddenly and forcibly realized. The words seemed to linger in the air as if searching for the objects of its hate. It was learned afterwards that his name was Dalton, a member of the steamfitters' union in Chicago. He was loudly applauded for his appropriate answer.

COIN rapped for order and continued:

"**We are not here to deal in sentiment—we are plain matter-of-fact people.**

QUANTITY SILVER IN THE WORLD.

"It is proposed by the bimetallists to remonetize silver, and add it to the quantity of money that is to be used for measuring the value of all other property.

"In dollars at a ratio to gold of sixteen to one, there are about the same number of dollars of silver in the world as gold. The report of the director of our mint says there was in the world in 1890, in the form of silver coin and bullion used as money, $3,820,571,346.

"A cubic foot of silver weighs 10,474 troy ounces, and using 371¼ grains to each dollar, this will make a cubic foot of cast silver worth $13,544.

"You get this by multiplying the 10,474 by 480, the number of grains in an ounce, and dividing the result by 371¼, the number of grains in a dollar. You then want to divide the $3,820,571,346, the silver of the world, by 13,544, the number of dollars in a cubic foot. It gives 282,085 cubic feet of silver in the world.

"Can you comprehend what a quantity of silver this is? I will tell you how. It will make a block of silver sixty-six feet wide, sixty-six feet long, and sixty-six feet high.

"You can put it all—all the silver of the world—in one of the rooms of this building, and anyone entering at the main entrance on Michigan avenue would have to inquire in which room of the building the silver of the world was, before he could find it.

"It will go in the Board of Trade room and still leave sufficient space, I imagine, for you gentlemen to do some business on dull days."

COIN now had the teller of the Metropolitan National Bank hand him a satchel containing one hundred and fourteen silver dollars. With these he showed that sixty-four silver dollars would lay down in eight rows, of eight each, in a square foot, and that one hundred and fourteen laid one upon the other measured a foot in height; that a cubic foot would therefore contain 7,296 silver dollars.

He then explained that the alloy (one-tenth), and the space between the sixty-four stacks of silver dollars, would hold the other $6,248 of the $13,544 in a solid cast cubic foot of pure silver.

He also stated that the gold and silver of the world obtainable for use as money, when mixed with its alloy and coined, could be stacked up in less than double the space it would occupy in solid cast blocks.

The little economist then continued: "All the silver in the world available for money can be stored in the room of the First National Bank of this city and the basement thereunder.

"This is the quantity of silver in the world, and it will be well for you to remember it when you hear some one talking about a flood of silver.

"We have heard a good deal about the treasury vaults at Washington groaning with silver, and more talk of enlarging them.

"The vaults under our treasury building can easily be arranged to hold all of the silver in all of the countries of the world used as money, either in coins, bars or bullion.

"You can empty all of the pockets of the people of the world of their silver, the bank vaults, the merchants' money drawers, the sub-treasuries, the children's safes, all India, Mexico, South America, England, France, Germany, Russia, Italy, Austria, the Netherlands, British America, China, Japan, and the islands, big and little, of the oceans, and you can put it all into this room, or in the basement of the Treasury building of the United States. [Applause]

"It is a matter of mathematical calculation and no intelligent citizen need be either alarmed or deceived."

With this statement COIN paused a moment, while people looked into each other's faces and back again at the speaker.

CHANGING THE MEASURE.

"Until 1873," he continued, "the primary money of the world was both silver and gold—at a parity. They were virtually one metal. The demand for primary money was met by the supply of both metals. The relative valuations of property to money, and money to property, adjusted themselves accordingly.

"Thus we had dollar wheat and 16-cent cotton in bimetallic measurement. A bushel of wheat went out into the market and purchased a dollar.

"Then came the abandonment of the use of silver as primary money by the United States, followed by Germany four months later, and then by the Latin Union, and recently by India.

"A new standard of measuring values was set up. Silver and gold combined was displaced by gold alone.

"Silver being deprived of this privilege—free coinage at the mints, and use as primary money—became property of the world, to have its value also measured in gold.

"As the standard for measurement in the countries making this change was now only one-half of what it had been, it meant the decline in value of all property.

"The demand for gold now became greater, and as other countries threw silver aside, the demand for gold still increased. It became more valuable—therefore, bought more property, silver included.

"As the effect of these changes began to be felt, prices declined. As the demand for gold increased, its value increased—just as the value of your wheat would increase if the double duty of both corn and wheat were put upon it.

"So the purchasing power of gold continued to increase—and this increase was indicated by what is known as the fall of prices. Silver was no longer primary money with us and it too as compared with *rising* gold declined in the market. It is the best thermometer we have to indicate the rise in gold.

"This scroll that I invite you to study," and here COIN unrolled a parchment and hung it on the wall, "gives you the decline in the price of silver, wheat, and cotton.

"We say 'decline,' but it would be equally true for us to say that these figures registered the *rise* in the purchasing power of money under this financial system that is based on gold.

"Our daily expression is that wheat or some other property has declined so much. Bradstreet and Dun reported last week an average decline in all property of one and 1-10 per cent.

"It would be a more intelligent understanding of the situation to say that the gold crop of the world—this crop that can be fenced in by twenty-two feet each way—had appreciated in value as the demand for it had increased.

"Remember that it has no way of expressing its value, except by what it will buy. The gold in a gold dollar may double or thribble in value, but so long as it is the unit of value, it will still be called a dollar, and when expressed in terms of money no increase in its value will be indicated.

"It only expresses its value in its purchasing power.

"If a dollar buys a bushel of wheat, during a time

Years	Bu. Wheat	Lb. Cotton	Oz. Silver
1872	1.40	18.0	1.32
1873	1.25	18.2	1.29
1874	1.35	15.0	1.27
1875	1.10	15.0	1.24
1876	1.20	12.9	1.15
1877	1.17	11.8	1.20
1878	1.30	11.1	1.15
1879	1.07	9.9	1.12
1880	1.25	11.5	1.14
1881	1.11	11.4	1.13
1882	1.19	11.4	1.13
1883	1.13	10.8	1.11
1884	1.07	10.5	1.01
1885	.86	10.6	1.06
1886	.87	9.9	.99
1887	.89	9.5	.97
1888	,85	9.8	.93
1889	.90	9.9	.93
1890	.83	10.1	1.04
1891	.85	10.0	.90
1892	.80	8.7	.86
1893	.63	7.0	.72

THE AVERAGE EXPORT PRICE OF WHEAT
COTTON AND SILVER FOR EACH YEAR
Named, as measured in GOLD

when the supply of wheat is normal, and the conditions continuing normal, at a later time a dollar will buy two bushels of wheat—then the dollar has doubled its purchasing power.

"We speak of declining prices, and do not think of the appreciation of gold. We speak of the sun coming up in the morning and going down in the evening. It is we that come up and go down. The sun is relatively fixed.

"Property is standing still and gold is going up.

"It is common now to hear the expression that the silver in a silver dollar is only worth sixty cents, or fifty cents, or forty-eight cents, as the case may be at the time. People do not stop to think what measure that value is being taken in. When we had a double standard, and silver was the *unit*, such a thing as its being worth less than a dollar was as impossible as it would be now for the gold in a gold dollar to be worth less than a dollar. Had gold been destroyed as primary money by the same nations, and silver made the standard, we could have had gold in the form of token money to-day, worth, say, fifty cents on the dollar as measured in silver.

AN ILLUSTRATION.

"Suppose both were destroyed as primary money, and a new standard of values was set up—and that standard was *diamonds*. Suppose a *carat* diamond was made the dollar or unit.

"And suppose gold and silver token money was used, of the weight and fineness now made, redeemable in this new redemption money.

"Under a double standard of silver and gold a pure *one-carat* diamond was rated at $50.00.* A change therefore to the diamond standard, would contract values fifty times. Wheat under a double standard that was worth $1.00 on the farms, would under like conditions with a diamond standard, be worth two cents as expressed in the new standard, or diamond dollar. It could then be said that the gold in a gold dollar, and the silver in a silver dollar

* Importers price before duty is paid.

was worth only about two cents. The demand for diamonds would become enormous, but as expressed in dollars a *carat* diamond would be a dollar. As expressed in purchasing power, it would buy fifty bushels of wheat. Wheat would be worth about two cents per bushel.

"Let me demonstrate. Say a *one-carat* diamond is now worth under a gold standard $25.00. If a *carat* diamond was adopted as the unit of value for our monetary system—*one-carat* declared by our law to be a *dollar*, and diamonds the only money of redemption, you would not say that a *carat* diamond was worth $25.00; but you would say that it was *one dollar*, or was worth one dollar.

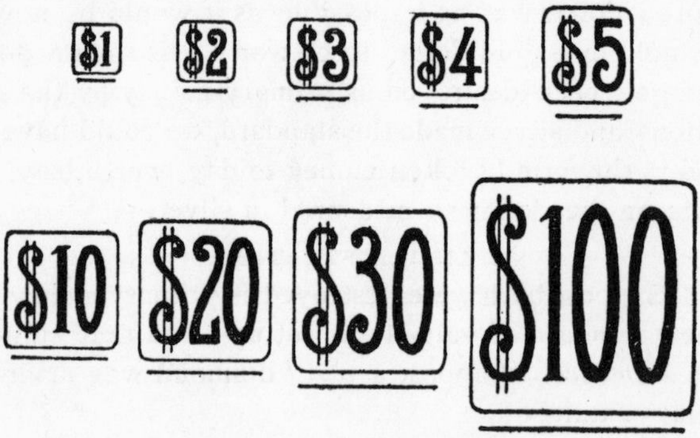

THE DIAMOND STANDARD.

"As expressed in dollars and cents it would pull everything down with it. Wheat now worth fifty cents would be worth one twenty-fifth of fifty, or two cents.

"You could then make fun of gold as some of our papers are now doing with silver, and say that the gold in a gold dollar was only worth two cents. It could be urged as a reason for not remonetizing gold with as much force as the same argument is now used against remonetizing silver. [Applause.]

"Those who have been deceived by this cry of a fifty-cent silver dollar have only themselves to blame, and if they are not money lenders 'they have been paying the fiddler.'

ANOTHER ILLUSTRATION.

"We express values in dollars, the unit of our monetary system. That unit is now the gold dollar of twenty-three and two-tenths grains of pure gold, or twenty-five and eight-tenths grains of standard gold. If we were to cut this amount in two and make eleven and six-tenths grains pure gold a *unit* or dollar, we would thereby double the value of all the property in the United States, except debts.

"If we were to double the weight of the *unit* or dollar by putting forty-six and four-tenths grains in it, we would thus reduce the value of all the property in the world, as expressed in dollars, except debts, as they call for so many dollars.

"If you don't understand this proposition as I have stated it, you will by enlarging the scale. Keep on adding gold to the dollar, till it takes one hundred grains—five hundred grains—one thousand grains—to make a legal *unit* or dollar. Go on making it larger till you have all of the gold in the world in one thousand *units*, or dollar pieces.

"Who could give up property enough to buy one of them? To buy a single dollar? Suppose you owed a note calling for $100.00 payable in gold, one-tenth the gold of the world—how could you pay it? Think of the property that would have to be slaughtered to get it.

"Carry the illustration still further and put all the gold in the world in one dollar. A note for one dollar would require all the gold to pay it. When you reduce the number of primary dollars, you reduce the value of

property as expressed in dollars accordingly, and make it that much more difficult for debtors to pay their debts.

ONE OF THE MEN WHO OWN THE GOLD

"And yet this is the kind of injustice that was committed when silver was demonetized. It struck down one-half the number of dollars that made up our primary money and standard of values for measuring the values of all property. It reduced the average value of silver and all other property one-half, except debts.

"It is commonly known as the *crime of 1873*. A crime, because it has confiscated millions of dollars worth of property. A crime, because it has made thousands of paupers. A crime, because it has made tens of thousands of tramps. A crime, because it has made thousands of suicides. A crime, because it has brought tears to strong men's eyes, and hunger and pinching want to widows and orphans. A crime, because it is destroying the honest yeomanry of the land, the bulwark of the nation. A crime, because it has brought this once great republic to the verge of ruin, where it is now in imminent danger of tottering to its fall. [Applause.]

ONE OF THE MEN WHO OWN THE COMMODITIES
SHERIFFS SALE

"Pardon me for an expression of feeling. We are not here to comment on the effects of demonetization, but to learn what money is, and wherein our financial system has been changed."

The little speaker, without intending it, through a feeling of honest indignation, had burst forth in a recital of this catalogue of crimes. It had a perceptible effect on the audience. His earnest eloquence was melting hearts that never before had thawed to the presentation of the subject.

It is one of the wonders of the world—how the people have been so slow in grasping the financial problem —in learning what it is that measures values, and that the lesson should have to be learned through an experience so bitter.

"And now," continued COIN, "if my explanation of what is known as the fifty-cent silver dollar is not plain and satisfactory I want to hear from you. It also accounts for fifty-cent wheat."

Mr. Ed. Pardridge, a noted bear operator on the Board of Trade, who had been listening attentively, here stood up. He had commenced bearing wheat in 1893, when it was 80 cents, and to the surprise of every one had continued confidently to sell it short down to 53½ cents, until he had made something like two millions of dollars and was still hammering away.

With a smile on his face and a wink all around him at his fellow members of the Board, he said:

"I have understood the relation of redemption money to values for now little over a year, and have profited by it; but you," addressing himself to COIN, "have given the snap away." Then amidst laughter and applause Mr. Pardridge took his seat.

Mr. Chas. Henrotin, a Board of Trade operator, then said that he had read in a morning paper, a statement signed by a Mr. Wheeler, that wheat in 1859 was as low as it is now, and as bimetallism was then the law, he would like to know how that was? Also that corn in 1873 was about the same price (38 cents) that it is now, and he would like to hear from COIN as to that point. Unless, he said, there is a satisfactory answer as to why corn was as low in 1873 as the present low price, he could not satisfactorily change his present views, which were for the gold standard.

COIN replied:

"The statement that wheat in 1859 was as low as now is not true.

"The secretary of your Board has the bound journals of a trade paper published in this city before the war that escaped the great fire. They are shown to any one who calls there. I have them here.

"They show that the average price of No. 2 red winter wheat for 1859 was $1.10 per bushel. The average price for the month of May, 1859, was $1.35.

"On this 11th day of May, (1859)," said COIN, turning to one of the books of the bound journals, "No. 2 Red wheat is here quoted at $1.38 and $1.40 per bushel. Wheat is now 54 cents a bushel; so this Mr. Wheeler is much mistaken when he says that wheat or anything else was as low in 1859 as it is now.

"We will take some other things," continued COIN. "I now hold in my hand the statistical abstract of the United States issued in 1892 by the Bureau of Statistics of the Treasury Department. Any of you can get it by writing to the treasury department. It brings the annual average prices down to 1892.

"On page 341 we see that the average price of cut nails in 1859 was, per 100 pounds, $3.86. In 1892, $1.83. Now they are about $1.00.

"On the same page the average price of pig iron in

1859 was $23.38 per ton. In 1892, $15.75; now it is about $12.00.

"On page 334 we find that the average price for 1859 of cotton was 12.08 cents per pound. In 1892, average price 7.71 cents per pound; now it is about 7 cents.

WHAT IT COSTS A FARMER TO DINE AT A FIRST-CLASS CHICAGO RESTAURANT.

"On page 335 we find the average price for 1859 of fine washed clothing, Ohio fleece wool, was 60 cents. For 1892, 30 cents.

"From this trade journal you will see that corn in 1859 was worth 65 cents.

"All other values on an average have declined like these I have just read. So you see that prices were not as low in 1859, or before the war, as they are now.

"Now, as to that part of your question as to the low price of corn in 1873," said COIN, looking toward Mr. Henrotin.

"What you say about the price of corn in 1873 is true; but I want to call your attention to the cause of it.

"Corn does not seek distant markets like wheat This is partly on account of its small price per bushel. It cannot always stand the freight. Its use is not so general as wheat, and it seeks the home market.

"On page 215 of the report of the Chicago Board of Trade for 1892 you will find that the corn crop of the State of Illinois, for the year 1872, which controlled the market price for the spring and summer of 1873, was 217,628,000 bushels; while by this year's report the crop for 1893 which controls the present price, was 160,-550,470 bushels. The demand for corn now, with nearly double our population, is greater than it was in 1873, and yet in 1873 the corn crop was fifty-seven million bushels greater in this state than it was last year. This over-production in 1872 accounts for its low price in 1873. The gold standard accounts for its low price now.

THE DEBTS OF THE WORLD.

Mr. H. F. Eames, president of the Commercial National Bank, put this question to COIN:

"Suppose values do decline and get on a lower plane. Can't the farmer who gets 50 cents for his wheat buy as much of this world's goods with that 50 cents as he formerly could with a dollar? And if this is true, and I think it is, wherein does it make any difference?"

And he sat down thinking he had accomplished what Professor Laughlin, Mr. Gage, Mr. Kirk and a dozen others had failed to do, viz., stump the little speaker.

He probably got the cleanest knockout and hardest fall of them all.

COIN turned to one of the boys who had helped to measure off the twenty-two feet in the corner and gave him some direction.

AN OBJECT-LESSON.

The boy went out into the anteroom, and a moment later returned, rolling a rubber globe or ball before him about half the size of the largest one on the platform. The people moving to make way, the lad rolled it to where COIN was standing. The little schoolmaster putting his hand on it, said:

"This ball, as proportioned to the largest one, indicates the debts of the world, which are, if we include debts of all kinds, about 200,000 million of dollars at the present time. The total value of all the property of the world in 1890 was about 450,000 million.

"This value has since been shrinking, and will continue to shrink until it is about one-half its present size as represented by this largest ball.

"But this ball that represents debts will not decrease any. Its present tendency is to grow larger.

"When this ball," indicating the one representing values of all property, "has shrunken to half its size, it will be about the size of this one representing debts.

"The history of nations shows that when the debts of a country are two-thirds of the value of all its property, disintegration sets in. Strikes—riots—revolution—provisional governments, as with our neighbors in South America at the present time.

"When you reduce wheat to 50 cents, and all other property accordingly, you don't reduce debts at all. You only make it harder to pay them.

A note executed five years ago which 1,000 bushels of wheat would then have paid, now takes about 1,500 bushels to pay.

Though we have paid since 1869 about 5,000 millions on our public debt in principal and interest, and have reduced the principal from 2,700 million to 1,000 million, it will now take as much of our property to pay the 1,000 million as would have paid the whole 2,700 million in 1869.

"A farmer may buy calico with his 50-cent wheat

money at a like cut in values, but he cannot get the same favor shown him on his debts.

"The property of the money lender—notes, bonds and mortgages—does not shrink. The mortgage will eat the property owner up.

"'Ah!' you may say, 'everybody is not in debt; one-half of the people may be, but let them liquidate and start over, then times will be good.'

"But everybody, except the money lender, *is in debt.* Your city is in debt twenty million, and you owe your part of it. Your county is in debt. Your state is in debt. Your general government is in debt.

"You are paying your part of the interest on all that; and your taxes in this city at the rate of 8 per cent on the assessed valuation is evidence that you are *all* in debt.

"Those who are personally in debt will only become bankrupt the sooner.

"The total debts in the United States, national, municipal, state, county, corporate and private, is now estimated to be about 40,000 million of dollars.

"The railroad bonded debt is 5,000 million, or about one-eighth of the whole amount.

"The interest on 40,000 million, at an average rate of 6 per cent per annum, is 2,400 million. Now, when you consider that the total money supply of the country is only about 1,600 million, and that interest money is going principally to the East, you can see what a great sponge this debt is, to come West twice a year and soak up your money and take it away.

"When your neighbor has sent all of his money off he has none left to spend with you.

"There are two ways ordinarily of getting this money back that goes East. One is to sell something to them at a profit. We are not now doing that. The other is to borrow it. So many of our friends have borrowed, that while they cannot borrow any more, it has made it unprofitable for those who can borrow to do so, as no business ventures are now profitable.

"The only money coming back to us at present from the East, which first goes there to pay interest, is about one hundred and sixty million a year paid by the government in pensions; salaries paid to government employés, and money received in payment for produce on which there is no margin or profit.

"On one hand the law of the land says these debts must be paid, and there are the courts and sheriffs to enforce it.

"On the other hand, the people cannot pay, as a new monetary unit makes it impossible. The law spends its force by confiscating the property of the people. The people will retaliate * * *. Under the effects of this legalized robbery, which has been in operation for twenty years, the future of the republic looks serious and threatening.

"While not directly interested in our neighbor's debts, we are indirectly; and general paralysis may come to our business on that account.

"In adjusting ourselves to a lower plane of prices, we are at once confronted with the fact that debts do not depreciate with other property, and that on account of its great size it becomes an oppression affecting all, more or less, and directly confiscating the property of millions.

"To expect these debts to be paid under present conditions, when it is so far beyond the power of the people to pay them, is too much. It is like trying to fit a 6-foot man to a 3-foot coffin. It will mutilate the remains to attempt it.

"Many other things do not, also, readily adjust themselves to a lower plane of prices.

"Suppose the proposition embraced in the question to me was made to the now irritated farmers, and one of

OUR DEBTS LIKE A GREAT SPONGE COME WEST AND SOAK UP THE MONEY.

them was to go forth to test it, and see if he could buy as much of this world's goods with 50 cents as he formerly could with a dollar.

"We will suppose, before starting, he goes to pay his taxes. He will find that his 50-cent wheat will not pay as much as his $1.40 wheat did in 1873. He will find his taxes just as much, and it will take all of twice as much wheat to pay them as in 1873.

"While passing out of the Court House suppose he meets a county official and should ask him what salary was paid to his office in 1873 and now. The answer would be the same number of dollars now as in 1873. The same is true of city, state and national officers, also with the army, navy and officials abroad. The 50-cent wheat would only pay about one-third as much in each instance. He starts for the depot and to get there he takes a street-car. He finds the fare the same as in 1873. He gets on a Pullman car to find the cost the same as in 1873. He registers at a first-class hotel. He finds the cost about the same as in 1873. He sends a telegram, and finds it costs the same as in 1873. He gets a shave with the same result. He buys tea and coffee, with the same result. He gets back home and goes to his bank to borrow money. He finds interest, except in cities on first-class loans, about as high as in 1873. Should he now meet the man who told him that his 50-cent wheat would buy as much of this world's goods as it ever did, it might result seriously for the other fellow." [Laughter and applause.]

And with a smile and a graceful bow COIN retired from the stage. The lecture was over. It had been full of "meat," and the bulls and bears knew more than they did before. If they had learned nothing else than that all of the gold and silver in the world could be put in the main room of the Chicago Board of Trade their attendance on the lecture gave rich returns for the time spent. The bears on the Board the next day were more numerous than they had been in many months.

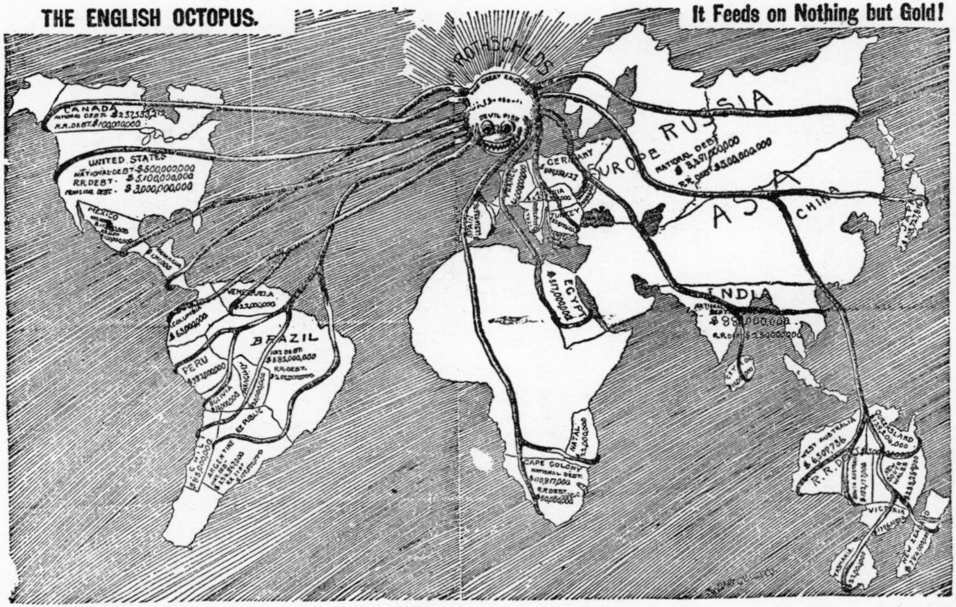

Denver Road.

"The Rothschilds own 1,600,000,000 in gold."—*Chicago Daily News.* This is nearly one-half the gold in the Chicago wheat pit.

A PARABLE.

A mother quail with her young quail brood had a home in a wheat field. When the wheat was ripe and the harvest time was come, the little quails suggested to their mother that it was time to move. While they were discussing it, the owner of the field came near, and was heard to say to some one with him, that he was going to get his neighbors to help him harvest. The mother quail said to her young, "We will not move yet." Several days passed by and the wheat had grown very ripe, The quail again heard the owner say that he was going after some friends over in another neighborhood, to help him cut the wheat. The mother quail said to her young, "We will not move yet." A few days later, when the wheat was so ripe it was falling and going to waste, the quails heard the farmer say, "I am going to cut the wheat myself." The mother quail then said to her young: "Now we will move. The wheat is to be cut."—*From an old Scrap Book.*

CHAPTER VI.

The Sixth Day.

The manner in which the little lecturer had handled his subject on the fifth day had greatly enhanced his popularity. What he had said, had been in the nature of a revelation to nearly all that heard it, and his grouping of facts had made a profound impression.

What created the most comment, was his statement as to the space in which all the gold and silver of the world could be placed. In all the hotel lobbies it was the subject of conversation. The bare statement that all the gold in the world could be put in a cube of 22 feet appeared ridiculous—absurd.

Few that had entertained the single gold standard view of the monetary question were willing to believe it. They argued that it was impossible ; that the business of the world could not be transacted on sucn an insignificant amount of property for primary money. They said, "Wait till the morning papers come out ; the *Tribune* would puncture it, the *Inter Ocean*, *Herald*, in fact, all of the papers would either admit it by their silence, contradict it or give the facts."

At the Grand Pacific Hotel the cashier was kept busy answering requests to see a twenty-dollar gold piece. They wanted to measure it—to get its diameter and thickness. As none was to be had, they had to content themselves with measuring up silver dollars and figuring out how much space all the silver in the world would occupy. This resulted in confirming COIN'S statement.

Mr. George Sengel, a prominent citizen of Fort Smith, Arkansas, while discussing the subject with a large party in the rotunda of the Palmer House, stood up in a chair and addressed the crowd, saying:

"Gentlemen, I have just been up in COIN'S room and examined the government reports as to the amount of gold and silver in the world, and have made the calculation myself as to the quantity of it, and I find that the statements made are true. All the gold and silver in the world obtainable for money can be put in the office of this hotel, and all the gold can be put in this office and not materially interfere with the comfort of the guests of the house.

"I have been until to-day in favor of a single gold standard, but hard times, and this fact that all the gold in the world available for money can be put in a space of twenty-two feet each way, has knocked it out of me. Count on me and old Arkansas for bimetallism."

Mr. Sengel's speech was greeted with applause, and he was followed by others expressing similar views.

The morning papers gave full reports of the previous day's lecture. All editorially confirmed COIN'S statement as to the quantity of gold and silver in the world, and the space it would occupy, except the *Herald* and *Tribune;* they were silent on the subject.

It was generally known that COIN would discuss independent action of the United States on the last day, and from the number that tried to gain admission, a hall many times as large could have been easily filled.

At the hour for opening the hall large crowds sur-

A brutal assault is made by a ruffian upon "Prosperity," a beautiful woman, in the sight of a prisoner, who trys to **break** his chains that he may go to her rescue.

rounded the entrance to the Art Institute, and the corridors were filled with people. In the large hall where the lectures were delivered the walls had been decorated with the American colors. This had been seen to by a committee of bimetallists; they had given special attention to the decorations around the platform, and though assuming many forms, each piece had been made from United States' flags. The scene presented was striking and patriotic.

When the doors were opened the hall was soon filled and thousands were turned away.

COIN was escorted by a committee of bimetallists in carriages from his hotel to the Art Institute, each carriage used by the committee being draped in the American colors. It was the first demonstration of the kind made in honor of the little financier of the people, since the lectures had begun.

The evidences of his popularity were now to be seen on every hand. Many, however, had reserved their judgment to hear from him on the United States taking independent action, and all were anxious to listen to what he would say on that subject.

His appearance upon the platform was the signal for an ovation. He had grown immensely popular in those last five days.

He laid his silk hat on the table, and at once stepped to the middle of the platform. He raised his eyes to the audience; slowly turned his head to the right and left, and looked into the sea of faces that confronted him.

INDEPENDENT FREE COINAGE.

"In the midst of plenty, we are in want," he began.

"Helpless children and the best womanhood and manhood of America appeal to us for release from a bondage that is destructive of life and liberty. All the nations of the Western Hemisphere turn to their great sister republic for assistance in the emancipation of the people of at least one-half the world.

"The Orient, with its teeming millions of people, and France, the cradle of science and liberty in Europe, look to the United States to lead in the struggle to

"IN THE MIDST OF PLENTY WE ARE IN WANT."

roll back the accumulated disasters of the last twenty-one years. What shall our answer be? [Applause.]

"If it is claimed we must adopt for our money the metal England selects, and can have no independent choice in the matter, let us make the test and find out if it is true. It is not American to give up without trying. If it is true, let us attach England to the United States and blot her name out from among the nations of the earth. [Applause.]

"A war with England would be the most popular ever waged on the face of the earth. [Applause.] If it is true that she can dictate the money of the world, and thereby create world-wide misery, it would be the most just war ever waged by man. [Applause.]

"But fortunately this is not necessary. Those who would have you think that we must wait for England, either have not studied this subject, or have the same interest in continuing the present conditions as England. It is a vain hope to expect her voluntarily to consent. England is the creditor nation of the globe, and collects hundreds of millions of dollars in interest annually in gold from the rest of the world. We are paying her two hundred millions yearly in interest. She demands it in gold; the contracts call for it in gold. Do you expect her to voluntarily release any part of it? It has a purchasing power twice what a bimetallic currency would have. She knows it.

"The men that control the legislation of England are citizens of that country with fixed incomes. They are interest gatherers to the amount annually of over one thousand millions of dollars. The men over there holding bimetallic conventions, and passing resolutions, have not one-fifth the influence with the law-making power that the bimetallists in the United States have with our Congress and President. No; nothing is to be expected from England.

"Whenever property interests and humanity have come in conflict, England has ever been the enemy of human liberty. All reforms with those so unfortunate as to be in her power have been won with the sword. She yields only to force. [Applause.]

"The money lenders in the United States, who own substantially all of our money, have a selfish interest in maintaining the gold standard. They, too, will not yield. They believe that if the gold standard can survive for a few years longer, the people will get used to it—get used to their poverty—and quietly submit.

"To that end they organize international bimetallic committees and say, 'Wait on England, she will be forced to give us bimetallism.' Vain hope! Deception on this subject has been practiced long enough upon a patient and outraged people.

"With silver remonetized, and gold at a premium, not one-tenth the hardships could result that now afflict us. Why? First: it would double the value of all property. Second: only 4 per cent of the business of the people of this nation is carried on with foreign countries; and a part of this 4 per cent would be transactions with silver using nations; while 96 per cent of the business of our people is domestic transactions, Home business. Is it not better to legislate in the interest of 96 per cent of our business, than the remaining 4 per cent?

"We now face the situation and *must* act. We are similarly situated to the Rocky Mountain bear hunter, when meeting a bear in a level trail on a mountain side, with a cliff on the one hand and a perpendicular precipice on the other. This Rocky Mountain bear hunter could neither dodge to the right or left, and there was no friendly tree near, his only weapon his knife, and no alternative but to fight. "It was to be the bear fight of his life. He knelt down and made this prayer, while the bear looked on with curiosity:

ROCKY MOUNTAIN BEAR HUNTER'S PRAYER.

"Oh Lord! I am now forty years of age, and I never prayed to Thee before in all my life. I am not like the Methodist and Baptist, who are constantly worrying Thee with all their little cares. All I have to say is, if you are not on my side don't be on the bear's side, but lay low and say nothing, and see the biggest bear fight you ever read about." [Great laughter.]

"In the impending struggle for the mastery of the commerce of the world, the financial combat between England and the United States cannot be avoided if we are to retain our self-respect, and our people their freedom and prosperity. [Applause.]

"The gold standard will give England the commerce and wealth of the world. The bimetallic standard will make the United States the most prosperous nation on the globe. [Applause.]

"To avoid the struggle means a surrender to England. It means more—it means a tomb raised to the memory of the republic. Delay is dangerous. At any moment an internecine war may break out among us. Wrongs and outrages will not be continuously endured. The people will strike at the laws that inflict them.

"To wait on England is purile and unnecessary. Her interests are not our interests. 'But,' you ask me, 'how are we to do it?' It will work itself. We have been frightened at a shadow. We have been as much deceived in this respect as we have about other matters connected with this subject.

"Free coinage by the United States will at once establish a parity between the two metals. Any nation that is big enough to take all the silver in the world, and give back merchandise and products in payment for it, will at once establish the parity between it and gold. [Applause.]

"France and the Latin Union, with less population and wealth than we have, maintained a premium on silver for forty years by opening their mints to its free coinage, and at a ratio of 15½ to 1, while ours was 16 to 1.

"If France could lift the commercial value of silver above that fixed by the other nations of the world, and at a premium over gold, the United States can hold its commercial value at a par with gold.

"But we alone would not have to maintain it. We know now that Mexico, South and Central America, the Asiatic governments and France would be with us from the start. The nations that would immediately support bimetallism are stronger in 1894, than those were in 1873 that maintained it then. Of all those that we had then, we would start with only the loss of Germany and Austria, and a few lesser principalities." [Applause.]

Mr. Lyman Gage, president of the First National Bank, who put questions to COIN on the second day of the school, now interrupted the speaker.

"Suppose," said Mr. Gage, "that after all, the independent action of the United States did not establish the parity between the two metals?"

"Why hesitate at the supposition of an improbability," replied COIN. Continuing he said:

"To suppose that such will be the case is to borrow trouble that is not at all likely to occur. But if it does, we are more fruitful of resources than are the obstacles insurmountable that may be thrown in our way.

"To begin with, we would want an administration at Washington that is friendly to republican institutions.

"The government should exercise its prerogative as of old to pay in either metal it sees fit. Gold must be given to understand that it is not indispensable to the currency of the country. This will depreciate its importance. The bankers of the great money centers must be given to understand that they must take their hands off the throat of the government. That they cannot dictate to the government what is money. The government will dictate that to them. The selfishness of the few must submit to the interests of the many. We will then be better able to dictate to other governments what the United States wants as she leads in the column of bimetallic nations.

"The unlimited demand for silver, and its free use by the government, will appreciate its value. To that extent the disuse of gold will depreciate *its* value. If

WHAT OUR ANSWER TO ENGLAND SHOULD BE.

necessary, fire a man bodily into the street to teach him his place. Gold needs that lesson.

"With both metals as primary money, property advances to bimetallic values, whether gold goes to a premium or not. Gold may go out of circulation, but its doing so does not disturb the practical effect of bimetallic prices.

"There should be a law making it a forfeiture of the debt to discriminate in favor of one form of national currency as against another. Our national currency should be as sacred as our national flag. The present law allowing gold to be named in the bond is statutory treason. The government would stand ready to redeem its paper and token money in primary money on demand, and should not allow any discrimination that would forestall its action or corrupt its financial system.

"With an administration in sympathy with bimetallism there would be no trouble as to the parity of the two metals. It could throw its great influence in favor of the weaker of the two metals if necessary in sustaining that parity."

"But," said Mr. Gage, "if after a fair trial gold continued at a premium, what remedy would you suggest?

"Put less gold in the gold dollar," replied COIN. "Bring the weight of the gold dollar down till they *are* on a parity." [Applause.]

Mr. Gage took his seat, but when COIN was about to resume he again interrupted the little speaker.

"Suppose" said Mr. Gage, "the free coinage of silver by the United States should flood us with silver? What would we do with it?"

"Put it in the pockets of the people" replied COIN. "Put it to work; put it in the channels of trade. If we desired to store it, we could put it all in your bank. [Applause.]

"But it would drive out our gold?" asserted Mr. Gage.

"Our gold is leaving us now," replied COIN. "Could it leave us any faster? It is now going the rate of from $500,000 to $2,000,000 a day. Is a drought of gold to be more desired than a flood of silver? It is only a question of time under a gold system when England will take it all. The way to keep our gold is to remonetize silver. Remonetization will give us higher prices for our exports, and will make a balance of trade in our favor large enough to bring us English gold and silver.

"Now, Mr. Gage," said COIN, "may I ask you a question?"

"Certainly," replied Mr. Gage.

"Is it not a fact," said COIN, "that no estimate has been placed on American (United States) bonds held in Europe at less than 5,000 million dollars?"

"Yes, I believe that is true," answered Mr. Gage.

"And is not the largest part of this sum owned in England?" continued COIN.

"I suppose it is," answered Mr. Gage.

"And has not," said COIN "the large shipments of gold to England recently given rise to the opinion in commercial circles that our bonds are held there to a larger amount than 5,000 million dollars.

"Yes," said Mr. Gage.

"Does not these securities," COIN went on, "consist largely of railroad, municipal and other bonds drawing from 4 to 6 per cent interest?"

"I suppose so," assented the banker.

"Then would you not," said COIN, "consider 4 per cent as a fair average interest on our bonds held in England?"

"Yes, I should think so," replied Mr. Gage.

"Mr. Gage" said COIN, "4 per cent on 5,000 million dollars is 200 million dollars. It has all been made payable in gold. The total production of gold in the world annually is about 165 millions, and of this the United States produces annnally about 35 millions. Now unless the balance of trade is increased largely, how may we expect to pay this 200 millions in gold annually?"

"The selling of more bonds in England will get us gold with which to pay it," replied the eminent financier.

"But does not that increase the annual interest to be paid?" asked COIN.

"Yes," said Mr. Gage, reluctantly.

"And where will it end?" continued COIN.

"I don't know," hesitatingly replied Mr. Gage, and with bewilderment in his face he resumed his seat.

COIN now addressed himself to the audience, that showed evident signs of pleasure and satisfaction with the dialogue that had just taken place.

"We have put our head in the mouth of the English lion, and the question now is how to get it out. I don't like Mr. Gage's plan. [Applause.]

"His plan consists in putting our heads farther in. [Applause.]

"It is the same plan the bankers have adopted for the government to get gold. [Applause.] It will all end, if the present policy is continued, in England owning us body and soul. She is making a peaceable conquest of the United States. What she failed to do with shot and shell in the eighteenth century, she is doing with the gold standard in the nineteenth century. [Applause.] The conservative monied interest furnished the tory friends of England then, and it furnishes her friends now. [Applause.] The business men of New York City passed strong resolutions against the Declaration of Independence in 1776, and they are passing strong resolutions against an American policy now." [Applause.]

"The objection to independent bimetallism is that the parity between the two metals cannot be maintained at our ratio of 16 to 1. That is—the gold (23.2 grains) in the gold dollar will be worth more than the silver (371¼ grains) in the silver dollar. We have twice changed the quantity of gold in the gold dollar; each time making it less. If the commercial value of 23.2 grains of gold is more than the commercial value of 371¼ grains of silver, then reduce it to 22, 21, 20 grains or less if necessary to put the two at a ratio, where the practical effect of free coinage, when once set to working again, will demonstrate that the ratio is at its natural point, and parity easily obtained. Reducing the gold in the gold dollar would leave gold for more dollars, and this would assist in establishing rising prices as it would multiply the number of dollars. The weight of the silver dollar should not be changed. Its integrity should be preserved as originally fixed.

"There can be no objection to this plan, for as we have seen the parity of the two metals was maintained for hundreds of years. The bimetallists do not believe that the ratio has much influence. They believe that the influence of unlimited free coinage is so great in establishing the commercial parity of the two metals, that any ratio near the natural ratio of 1 to 15⅔ will give satisfaction.

"In this controversy, one point should never be lost sight of, and that is, that higher prices—*bimetallic* prices—will come with remonetization of silver, even though gold goes to a premium.

"It is a fixed law in the science of money that when both metals are *primary money—whether at the time seeking the mints or not, and whether in circulation or not—bimetallic prices prevail.*

Mr. P. A. H. Franklin, a prominent bimetallist of Chicago, wanted to know of COIN, in case it was necessary or desirable, if there were any practical method to force England to adopt bimetallism?

COIN'S reply was: "Yes. It is not probable that such an emergency can arise; but if it does all we would have to do would be to put an excessive tariff on all imports coming from her, and all other countries having a gold standard, until they adopted a bimetallic system with the same ratio as ours.

"England could not afford to stay out of our markets while France was enjoying them. The English people would raise a clamor that would soon lead to bimetallism. If such a course on our part conflicts with treaties—treaties should be broken. When humanity, or the life of a nation, is involved, all treaties are at an end.

"If England wages a war on humanity, the United States should declare an industrial war on England. [Applause.]

"England demonetized silver in 1816, and yet from that period to 1873 the parity of the two metals was not affected; we did not need her then, and we do not need her now.

"When the nations giving importance to silver, are as numerous and as strong as those giving importance to gold, a parity is naturally produced.

"The farmer in Mexico sells his bushel of wheat for one dollar. The farmer in United States sells his bushel of wheat for 50 cents. The former is proven by the history of the world to be an equitable price. The latter is writing its history, in letters of blood, on the appalling cloud of debt that is sweeping with *ruin* and *desolation* over the farmers of this country. [Applause.] What is said of wheat may be said of all our property.

"When it is considered that we are giving two dollars worth of property now, in payment for one dollar in gold, you will realize that we are now paying 100 per cent premium on gold. [Applause.]

"And this applies not only to our foreign business, but to our home business.

"With silver remonetized, and a just and equitable standard of values, we can, if necessary, by act of Congress, reduce the number of grains in a gold dollar till it is of the same value as the silver dollar. [Applause.] We can legislate the premium out of gold. [Applause.] Who will say that this is not an effective remedy? I pause for a reply!"

COIN waited for a reply. No one answering him, he continued:

"Until an answer that will commend itself to an unbiased mind is given to this remedy, that guarantees a parity between the metals, write upon the character of every 'international bimetallist' the words '*gold monometallist.*'"

Pausing for a moment, as if still waiting for his position to be attacked, he proceeded:

"Give the people back their favored primary money! Give us two arms with which to transact business! Silver the right arm and gold the left arm! Silver the money of the people, and gold the money of the rich.

"Stop this legalized robbery, that is transferring the property of the debtors to the possession of the creditors!

"Citizens! the integrity of the government has been violated. A Financial Trust has control of your money, and with it, is robbing you of your property. Vampires feed upon your commercial blood. The money in the banks is subject to the check of the money lenders.

They expect you to quietly submit, and leave your fellow citizens at their mercy. Through the instrumentality of law they have committed a crime that overshadows all other crimes. And yet they appeal to law for their protection. If the starving workingman commits the crime of trespass, they appeal to the law they have contaminated, for his punishment. Drive these money-

GREED.

changers from our temples. Let them discover by your aspect, their masters—the people." [Applause.]

"The United States commands the situation, and can dictate bimetallism to the world at the ratio she is inclined to fix.

"Our foreign ministers sailing out of the New York harbor past the statue of "Liberty Enlightening the World" should go with instructions to educate the nations of the earth upon the American Financial Policy. We should negative the self-interested influence of England, and speak for industrial prosperity.

"We are now the ally of England in the most cruel and unjust persecution against the weak and defenseless people of the world that was ever waged by tyrants since the dawn of history. [Applause.]

"Our people are losing each year hundreds of millions of dollars; incalculable suffering exists thoughout the land; we have begun the work of cutting each others throats; poor men crazed with hunger are daily shot down by the officers of the law; want, distress and anxiety pervades the entire Union.

"If we are to act let us act quickly.

"It has been truthfully said:

"'It is at once the result and security of oppression that its victim soon becomes incapable of resistance. Submission to its first encroachments is followed by the fatal lethargy that destroys every noble ambition, and converts the people into cowardly poltroons and fawning sycophants, who hug their chains and lick the hand that smites them!'

"Oppression now seeks to enslave this fair land. Its name is greed. Surrounded by the comforts of life, it is unconscious of the condition of others. Despotism, whether in Russia marching its helpless victims to an eternal night of sorrow, or in Ireland where its humiliating influences are ever before the human eye, or elsewhere; it is the same.

"It is already with us. It has come in the same form that it has come everywhere—by regarding the interests of property as paramount to the interests of humanity. That influence extends from the highest to the lowest. The deputy sheriff regards the $4 a day he gets as more important to him than the life or cause of the workmen he shoots down.

"The Pullman Palace Car Company recently reduced the already low wages of its employés 33⅓ per cent. Unable to make a living, they laid down their tools. A few days later the company declared a quarterly dividend of 2 per cent on watered capital of $30,000,000. This quarterly dividend was $600,000.

"Had this company sent for the committee of the workmen and said, 'We were about to declare our regular quarterly dividend of 2 per cent; it amounts to $600,000; we have concluded to make it 1½ per cent; this will give us $475,000 for three months, or one quarter's profits, and we are going to use the other $125,000 to put back the wages of the men. There would have been no strike. The men would have hailed it as generosity, and the hearts of 4,000 workmen would have been made glad.

"It was not done. It was not to be thought of. These stockholders living in comfort with all their wants provided for, think more of their property interests than they do of humanity, and will see men starve or reduced to the condition of serfs rather than concede an equitable distribution of the profits of their business.

"This has occurred here in the city of your homes; in the World's Fair city; a city supposed to be as patriotic as any we have; if this is human nature here, what do you expect from the men in England who hold our bonds, notes and mortgages payable in gold.

"We are forced to take independent action. To hesitate is cowardly! Shall we wait while the cry of the helpless is heard on every hand? Shall we wait while our institutions are crumbling?" (Cries of "No —no—no!")

"This is a struggle for humanity. For our homes and firesides. For the purity and integrity of our government.

"That all the people of this country sufficiently intelligent to vote cannot understand that the reduction of our primary money to one half its former quantity reduces the value of property proportionately, is one of the inexplainable phenomena in human history.

"Those who do understand it should go among the people and awake them to the situation of peril, in which they are placed. Awake them as you would with startling cries at the coming of flood and fires.

"Arouse them as did Paul Revere as he rode through the streets shouting: 'The British are on our shores.'

"To let England dictate to us was not once the spirit of Americans.

"When Benjamin Franklin was minister to England he attended a banquet in London, at which, toasts were responded to by the Premier of England, and the ministers of France and the United States. The toast in each instance was the government represented by the official responding.

"The toast to England came first and was responded to by the Premier. He was eloquent in praise of his country, and at the close of his speech took up his wineglass and said, 'Now drink with me again to England, the Sun that gives light to the world.'

"The toast to France came next, and the French minister did great justice to his subject. Imitating the English Premier he closed his address by lifting his wineglass high, and saying, 'Now drink again with me to

France, the Moon that controls the tides of the world.'

"As Mr. Franklin arose to respond to the toast—the *United States*—all eyes were upon him. The French minister had taken up the gage thrown down by the Premier of England and had responded fittingly as to the position of France among the nations of the earth. What would Mr. Franklin say? Would he properly acquit himself for the United States?

"At the close of an able response, suitable to such an occasion, Mr. Franklin placed his hand on his wine-glass, and lifting it to a level with his eyes, said: 'Now drink with me again to the United States, the Joshua that commanded the sun and moon to *stand still*, and they *stood still*.' [Applause.]

"Had Mr. Franklin had the ears of all the people of the United States on that occasion, one universal acclaim would have resounded throughout this land.

"If we had an administration and Congress now, that would say to England '*Stand still*'—one glad shout would be heard in this country from Sea to Sea and Lakes to Gulf, proclaiming the second independence of the United States." [Long continued applause.]

Coin had finished. The audience had risen to its feet, and the applause was tumultuous and continued. Those on the stage were shaking the little statesman's hands, and many others were crowding around the platform.

As the tumult subsided a fine-looking gentleman appeared on the platform with his hands raised to command attention. It was Mr. J. L. Caldwell, president of the First National Bank of Huntington, West Virginia. As soon as he had secured attention he said:

"I am the president of a national bank, and I want to first say to you people that all national bankers do not regard selfish personal interest, as paramount to love of country and the interests of the whole people.

"A few of us have stood out against this gold standard system, and are in favor of immediate free coinage, 16 to 1 or 15½ to 1, independent of England. [Applause.]

"I now propose *three cheers* for COIN."

They were given with a will. The *hip! hip! hurrahs!* were heard through the open windows for two squares away.

Thus ended the "school." Chicago has had its lesson on bimetallism.

How will this contest end?

No one can tell. In the struggle of might against right, the former has generally triumphed.

Will it win in the United States?

COIN RECEIVES.

The office and corridors of the Palmer House, at which Coin was stopping, were so crowded the afternoon and evening of the day the lectures closed by people anxious to see him, he was prevailed upon to give a reception, which he did the following day, and for hours the people filed through the parlors and shook the little statesman by the hand.

The reception was at times interrupted by distinguished men who desired to ask a question, and when this occurred, those near him would hear the reply, and a short-hand reporter of the *City Press* was at the table in the room taking down what was said.

The only thing that transpired that would interest the general reader were questions put by Senator S. M. Cullom of Illinois, and others.

Senator Cullom wanted to know what the little financier thought of the American coinage proposition: "To throw the mints of the United States open to the free coinage of silver produced in the United States only."

Coin replied: "To restate your proposition, Senator, it is to leave the mints of the United States open to the free coinage of the gold of the world, and to open them to the free coinage of the silver of this government only. Such a policy is good as far as it goes, but it does not go far enough to furnish a remedy. Such a policy leaves us at the mercy of gold standard countries in the settlement of balances with them. When the mints of this country, a powerful dominating government like this, are open to the free coinage of the silver of the world, at a ratio of, say 16 to 1, then the owner of silver bullion in a foreign country will not exchange his silver for gold at a cheaper ratio than he can get for it in the United States, less the cost of expressage or freight, in other words what is known as the cost of exchange. In exchange for gold, he will therefore demand and receive from his home market the ratio we establish. Thus, to throw open our mints to the silver *of the world* fixes the exchangeable value of the two metals the world over.

"The narrower, or 'American product' policy would drive away from us the trade of all silver-using nations whose silver was denied admission to our country. Such a policy would leave gold at a premium over silver, force us to pay gold in settlement with all gold standard countries, and alienate all silver-using countries from us, while England would roam the commercial world over, viewing with satisfaction our isolated policy. This too, is a larger and broader question. The debts in this country have been made payable in gold; it has been so written in the bonds and most of the notes. Foreigners hold our securities for more than $5,000,000,000, and our home creditors hold the balance. To establish a parity between the two metals enables us to exchange silver for gold, 16 for 1, and thus assists us to pay these debts. To coin the American product will not restore a parity or furnish relief. Absolute free coinage, as outlined in my lecture yesterday, forces a parity. The 'American product' proposition leaves us still shackled to the English policy, with our debts in their hands payable in gold at a premium over silver.

"We are," he continued, "the producers of silver, and to export it at a higher exchangeable value with gold and other commodities, means more wealth to flow to us. The broad policy, is for the United States to force the world, by her example and influence, to bimetallism, which is, as we have seen, easily in our power to do. We must put forth a counter influence to the gold standard influence of England, and once exerted, that influence is stronger than hers."

Mr. C. S. Collins, a prominent bimetallist of Little Rock, Ark., said the bankers were agitating a proposition that, if made a law, would allow the banks to issue paper money based on their credits, and thereby increase the volume of money very largely. It was, he said, what is commonly known as the plan of the Banker's convention. He wanted to know of the little financier if in his judgment it would afford relief.

"No," was the reply. "Such plan does not increase the stock of primary money—the measure of values—and would leave us a prey to the low prices that now exist. It is another proposition to deceive the people and divert their minds from the true remedy. *Our* proposition should be to *stand fast and refuse all compromises.* To enlarge the privileges the banks now have, is to place the people in a condition of more hopeless bondage to the money power. The bankers as a rule are a patriotic class of men, but they are controlled by a central influence in London and New York, the effect of which is fatal to the prosperity of the country."

Mr. W. Y. Miles, of Columbus, Ohio, a large, fine looking, wholesale merchant of that city, and a great admirer of Senator Sherman, shook hands with the little statesman and said that "Senator Sherman claimed that the decline in the value of silver bullion was not an account of demonetization, but by reason of the large over-production of silver as compared with gold, beginning with and since 1873, and that Senator Sherman's statement to that effect had been recently published through the associated press in all the daily papers. Is not this over-production of silver true?" concluded Mr. Miles. And as he said this the expression on his face was that of one well pleased with himself and the views he entertained, which were those of the gold monometallist.

The people in line, temporarily blocked by this interruption, pressed forward, and as many as could gathered near to hear the reply. It was true that Senator Sherman had made the statement, and from its recent publication it was then fresh in the minds of all present. The friends of silver listening were over-anxious as to the reply the little bimetallist would make. Could he settle effectually and forever a statement so damaging from such a high authority?

The fact that he had, both on the first and second days of his lectures, given figures from the table of Mulhall, the London Statistician, disproving this statement, was not known to Mr. Miles, and for the moment was not remembered by many present, but it was an English authority, and about its authenticity there might be some doubt, and probably would be, since the statement made by Mr. Sherman.

Mr. Miles' confidence in Senator Sherman, like

thousands of other American citizens, was unbounded, and he had no doubt of the truth of the statement made by the Ohio Senator.

He expected an evasive reply.

"Mr. Miles," said COIN, "I here hand you a copy of the third edition of my Hand Book, and open it for you at page 26. That page is a copy, figure for figure, from a page in the report of the Director of the Mint of the Treasury Department of the United States. It gives the production of the gold and silver of the *world* for 100 years; 1792 to 1892. It shows that for the first 50 years of this century the production of silver was largely in excess of gold. If you will compute the per centage, you will find that it is 78 per cent of silver over gold, and yet there was no trouble to maintain the commercial parity between the two metals during that period. Now replying direct to Senator Sherman's statement, I call your attention to the year 1873. For that year it shows gold $96,200,000, silver $81,800,000. For 1874, gold $90,750,000, silver $71,500,000. For 1875, gold $97,500,000, silver $80,500,000. These are the figures of the United States treasury department, Mr. Miles," said the little fellow, looking up into the face of the handsome Ohio merchant. And then he continued: "For 1876, gold $103,700,000, silver $87,-600,000. For 1877, gold $114,000,000, silver $81,000,000. For 1878, gold $119,000,000, silver $95,000,000." Here COIN handed him the book and told him to take it home with him and think over Senator Sherman's statement, and then added: "You will find by examining a more recent statement of the treasury department that extends this table down to the present, that while *during the first fifty years of this century the world produced 78 per cent more silver than gold, that during the last twenty-one years the production of silver over gold has been less than 5 per cent.* Write to the treasury department for this table," and as COIN said this he looked around at the people listening; then he added: "I want to see the treasury department flooded with letters for this information, and I want to see them furnish it; they are your servants and should do so, and with this official table in the possession of the people, I want them to try Senator Sherman for veracity, and inquire into the motive of him and others for making this and similar deceptive statements to the public."

And Mr. Miles and the line of callers passed on.

The page in COIN'S Hand Book referred to by COIN and shown to Mr. Myles, is as follows:

Production of Gold and Silver in the World, 1792-1892.

CALENDER YEARS.	GOLD.	SILVER (Coining Value).	TOTAL.
1792-1800 . . .	$106,407,000	$328,860,000	$435,267,000
1801-1810 . .	118,152,000	371,677,000	489,829,000
1811-1820 . . .	76,063,000	224,786,000	300,849,000
1821-1830 . . .	94,479,000	191,444,000	285,923,000
1831-1840 . . .	134,841,000	274,930,000	400,771,000
1841-1848 . . .	291,144,000	259,520,000	550,664,000
1849	27,100,000	39,000,000	66,100,000
1850	44,450,000	39,000,000	83,450,000
1851	67,600,000	40,000,000	107,600,000
1852	132,750,000	40,600,000	173,350,000
1853	155,450,000	40,600,000	196,050,000
1854	127,450,000	40,600,000	168,050,000
1855	135,075,000	40,600,000	175,675,000
1856	147,600,000	40,650,000	188,250,000
1857	133,275,000	40,650,000	173,925,000
1858	124,650,000	40,650,000	165,300,000
1859	124,850,000	40,750,000	165,600,000
1860	119,250,000	40,800,000	160,050,000
1861	113,800,000	44,700,000	158,500,000
1862	107,750,000	45,200,000	152,950,000
1863	100,950,000	49,200,000	156,150,000
1864	113,000,000	51,700,000	164,700,000
1865	120,200,000	51,950,000	172,150,000
1866	121,100,000	50,750,000	171,850,000
1867	104,025,000	54,225,000	158,250,000
1868	109,725,000	50,225,000	159,950,000
1869	106,225,000	47,500,000	153,725,000
1870	106,850,000	51,575,000	158,425,000
1871	107,000,000	61,050,000	168,050,000
1872	99,600,000	65,250,000	164,850,000
1873	96,200,000	81,800,000	178,000,000
1874	90,750,000	71,500,000	162,250,000
1875	97,500,000	80,500,000	178,000,000
1876	103,700,000	87,600,000	191,300,000
1877	114,000,000	81,000,000	195,000,000
1878	119,000,000	95,000,000	214,000,000
1879	109,000,000	96,000,000	205,000,000
1880	106,500,000	96,700,000	203,200,000
1881	103,000,000	02,000,000	205,000,000
1882	102,000,000	111,800,000	213,800,000
1883	95,400,000	115,300,000	210,700,000
1884	101,700,000	105,500,000	207,200,000
1885	108,400,000	118,500,000	226,900,000
1886	106,000,000	120,600,000	226,600,000
1887	105,775,000	124,281,000	230,056,000
1888	110,197,000	140,706,000	250,903,000
1889	123,489,000	162,159,000	285,648,000
1890	113,150,000	172,235,000	285,385,000
1891	120,519,000	186,733,000	307,252,000
1892	130,817,000	196,605,000	327,422,000
Total . . .	$5 633 908,000	$5,104,961,000	$10,738,869,00

TREASURY DEPT., BUREAU OF THE MINT, Aug. 16, 1893.

APPENDIX.

It will be noticed that during the lectures, COIN was never asked to answer the proposition of "*over-production.*" His attention was afterward called to this, and he replied: That he was not surprised; that under-prcduction was now conceeded by all who had investigated it, and the newspapers seldom mentioned it. That over-production could not be claimed so long as tens of thousands were going hungry; and that the only over-production admitted by all, was millionaires.

COIN used in his lectures the phrase "1 to 16" in speaking of ratio. This was used for convenience. The exact ratio is 1 to 15.98, but, as by common usage, the term 1 to 16 is used, the correct figures 1 to 15.98 would have been confusing.

The assessed valuation of all the property in the United States, as given by Census Bulletin No. 192, issued June 4, 1892, is $24,651,585,465.

In giving the debts of the United States, public, corporate and private, COIN has used in part the report of the Census Bureau, as far as completed, and has added to it an estimated amount for maritime debts, accounts, pawn shops, private debts not on record, rentals, and other debts due on contracts, none of which is included in the census report. Among the larger items of our debts, as far as officially reported, are the following:

National debt of the United States (U. S. Census, 1890	$ 891,960,104
State and Municipal debt (U. S. Census, 1890)	1,135,210,442
Railway bonds on 171,866 miles railway, 1892 (Poor's Manual, '93)	5,463,611,204
The average farm and home debt shown by tabulation of partial returns from counties distributed throughout the Union, is $1,288 for farm and $924 for homes. If this average holds good for the United States, there is an existing debt in force, on the farms and homes of the United States occupied by owner (R. B. Porter, Supt. 11th Census, in North American Review, Vol. 153, page 618) of	2,500,000,000
Mortgaged Indebtedness of Business Realty, Street Railways, Manufactories and Business enterprise(estimated from partial reports of 11th Census)	5,000,000,000
Loans from 3,773 National Banks (Statistical Abstracts of the United States)	2,153,769,806
Loans from 5,579 State, Saving, Stock and Private Banks and Trust Companies (Statistical Abstracts of the United States)	2,201,764,292

If the same progressive ratio of increase is added to these figures that maintained from 1880 to 1890, over 5,000 million should now be added to the items above given.

Taking the figures used by COIN in the Fifth Chapter, we find that the actual ratio between the two metals is 1 to $15\frac{2}{3}$.

The following is the calculation:

THE RATIO.

No. cubic feet gold in the world,	**No. cubic feet silver in the world,**	
9796	282085	
No. ounces in a cubic foot gold,	**No. ounces in a cubic foot silver,**	
19258	10474	
78368	1128340	
48980	1974595	
19592	1128340	
88164	282085	
9796		
188651368	2954558290	$15\frac{2}{3}$
	188651368	
	1068044610	
	943256840	
	124787770	

$$\frac{124787770}{188651368} = \frac{2}{3}$$

The ratio of the two metals as they exist in the world available for money is 1 to $15\frac{2}{3}$.

By making gold the only primary money, the natural result is to depress the *commercial* value of silver; this depression now marks a commercial ratio between the two metals of 1 to 33; sooner or later, on account of the large gold interest-bearing debt in this country, money will be concentrated in the money centers; values of all property will be further depressed, until the commercial ratio between gold and silver can be expected to go to 1 to 40 or more.

INDEX.

Crime of 1873 .... 105, 204
Commercial Value of Gold and Silver, how affected by Free Coinage 117–128
Credit money 141–156
Checks, effect of in diminishing quantity of money needed 146
Cotton, its decline since 1873 200
Cotton, price of in 1859 207
Coin puts questions to Mr. Gage 229

Demonetization, effect of 124, 130, 144
Demonetization, effect of on Silver Standard Countries 180
Diamond Standard 201
Debts of the World 208
Debts of the United States 211, 247–249
Debts, interest on, strangling prosperity 208–214

Evans, Mr., how he studied Political Economy 103
Eustis, P. S., asks a Question 161
Eames, H. F., President Commercial National Bank asks a Question 208
England, will not consent to Bimetallism, reason 222, 229
England—how to force her to adopt Bimetallism 232

Fifty-cent Silver Dollar explained 198–205
Franklin, P. A. H., asks a Question 232

Gold basis claimed since 1837, answered 99
Gold never the unit prior to 1873 101
Gold Dollar made smaller in 1834 .... 97, 115
(And again in 1837) 110
Gold and Silver, quantities in World compared at different periods 122
Gold, quantity of 129
Gold and Silver, why adopted as money 138
Gold Standard Countries all affected by Demonetization 178
Gold, quantity *per capita* in the World 190
Gold, of the World and space it will occupy 191
Gold, weight per cubic foot 191
Gold, value per cubic foot 191
Gold, number cubic feet in the World 192
Gold, of the World in the Chicago Wheat pit 192

Gold, its rise in value 199
Gold Dollar, its increase in size would lower values........... 203
Gold, premium now paid for it.............................. 233
Gage, Lyman, President First National Bank asks a Question. 115, 226
Gage, Lyman, makes an admission............................ 128
Greenback system of money.................................. 167

Hopkins, Mayor of Chicago, asks a Question...... 181
Henrotin, Chas., asks a Question........................... 205

Improved Facilities do not account for low prices............ 176
Independent *free coinage*................................ .. 228

Kirk, President Exchange National Bank, asks a Question.... 176
Kohlsaat, H. H., asks a Question 177

Lawson, Victor F., Jr., asks a Question...................... 108
Laughlin, Professor, asks a Question......................... 160
Latin Union, what Countries Constitute....................... 161

Medill, Mr., asks a Question................................. 99
Montgomery, J. A., Supt. of Mails, asks a Question........... 162
Money, necessity of.. 136
Money, a science 141–156
Money, primary 141–156
Money, credit 141–156
Money, quantity of in United States.......................... 145
Money, based on labor 170
Money, quantitative theory................................... 187
Money Lenders, why they favor a Gold Standard............. 223

Nails, price of in 1859....................................... 206

Parity, how maintained....................... 117–128, 225, 233
Primary money... 141–156
Panics, causes producing, explained and illustrated...... 147–156

Ratio.. 97, 115
Ratio, change in 97, 110, 115
Ratio, compared for two hundred years........................ 124
Ratio, commercial as affected by Demonetization.......... 124, 125
Ratio, why the change was made in the Gold and not in the Silver Dollar.. 130, 131
Rozett, Geo. H., asks a Question............................. 129
Ridgeley, E. R., asks a Question............................. 167
Rocky Mountain Bear Hunter's Prayer.......................... 224

Scott, Mr., asks a Question.................................. 102
Smith, Wm. Henry, Jr,, asks a Question 110

Scudder, M. L., Jr., asks a Question.................................. 165
Struckman, President County Commissioners, asks a Question. 172
Standard silver and gold explained.................................. 104
Silver in circulation prior to 1873.................................. 99, 100
Silver, foreign, made legal tender.................................. 99, 100
Silver, claimed to be so plentiful as to cease to be a precious metal, answered.................................. 108
Silver at a premium in 1873.................................. 109
Silver, none of the facts used in arguments against it now existed at the time it was Demonetization.................................. 109
Silver, when demonetized, in England, United States, Germany and the Latin Union.................................. 119
Silver, price of nineteen years before, and nineteen years after Demonetization.................................. 121
Silver and gold, quantities compared at different periods...... 122
Silver, quantity of..................................129, 187, 196
Silver, why it is not now money.................................. 129, 130
Silver and gold, why adopted as money.................................. 138
Silver, cost of producing.................................. 165
Silver states, not benefited by remonetization, except in common with the other states.................................. 172
Silver, the most constant standard of values.................................. 179
Silver of the World, space it will occupy.................................. 196
Silver, weight of a cubic foot.................................. 196
Silver, value of a cubic foot.................................. 196
Silver, number cubic feet in the world.................................. 196
Silver, its decline in value since 1873.................................. 200

Tariff, high or low, does not account for present depression.... 177

Unit.................................. 95, 96, 97, 101, 102, 104, 106
Unit, why fixed on silver.................................. 98
Unit, changed to gold in 1873.................................. 106

Walsh, John R., President Chicago National Bank, asks a Question.................................. 139, 146
Wheeler, D. H., asks a Question.................................. 145
Wheat, its decline in value since 1873.................................. 200
Wheat, price of in 1859.................................. 206
Wool, price of in 1859.................................. 207

Value, of silver and gold if both were Demonetized.......... 162
Value, of all property in the World.................................. 187
Value, of all property in United States,................ (Appendix)

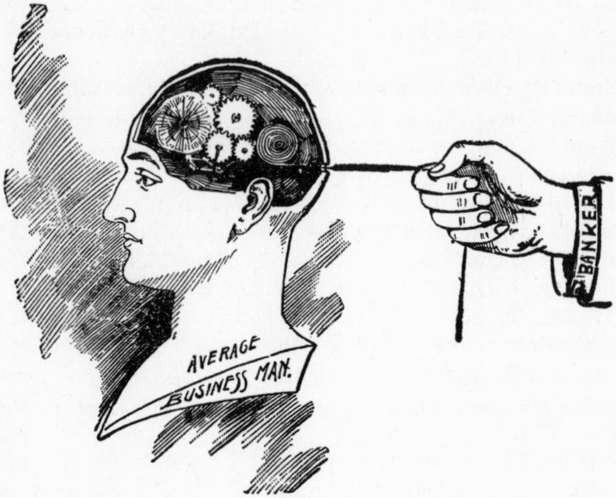
AVERAGE
BUSINESS MAN.
BANKER

THE JOHN HARVARD LIBRARY

The intent of Waldron Phoenix Belknap, Jr., as expressed in an early will, was for Harvard College to use the income from a permanent trust fund he set up, for "editing and publishing rare, inaccessible, or hitherto unpublished source material of interest in connection with the history, literature, art (including minor and useful art), commerce, customs, and manners or way of life of the Colonial and Federal Periods of the United States . . . In all cases the emphasis shall be on the presentation of the basic material." A later testament broadened this statement, but Mr. Belknap's interests remained constant until his death.

In linking the name of the first benefactor of Harvard College with the purpose of this later, generous-minded believer in American culture the John Harvard Library seeks to emphasize the importance of Mr. Belknap's purpose. The John Harvard Library of the Belknap Press of Harvard University Press exists to make books and documents about the American past more readily available to scholars and the general reader.

DATE DUE